Outsourcing For Success

How to Make the Most of Freelance Talent and Boost your Business

Kev Ashcroft

Copyright © 2021 by Kev Ashcroft. All rights reserved.

This book or any portion thereof may not be reproduced or used in any manner whatsoever without the express written permission of the publisher, except for the use of brief quotations in a book review.

Printed in the UK
First printing: 2021
ISBN: 979-8-5030214-1-7
Digital publisher: Kev Ashcroft
Hard copy publisher: Kev Ashcroft

Editing: Bryony Sutherland
Cover design: Blinkered Media
Typesetting: Blinkered Media

To the best wee Ma in the entire world.
A tower of strength and great spirit.
I hope as you look on from wherever you may be,
you're able to rest and smile.
Stay crazy wee Ma, stay crazy xx

Table of Contents

Preface **4**

Introduction **10**

Chapter 1: Why outsource? **15**
- *Benefits for business owners* *17*
- *Benefits for freelancers* *26*
- *Disadvantages for business owners* *33*
- *Disadvantages for freelancers* *35*
- *Managing expectations* *39*

Chapter 2: Case Studies **43**
- *FreeUp* *43*
- *The JAR Group* *45*

Chapter 3: Freelance Marketplaces A-Z **48**
- *CloudPeeps* *50*
- *Codeable* *53*
- *DesignCrowd* *58*
- *Envato Studio* *63*
- *Fiverr* *67*
- *Fivesquid* *71*
- *FlexJobs* *75*
- *FreeUp* *77*
- *Freelancer* *81*

Giggrabbers *84*
Guru *87*
PeoplePerHour *89*
Reedsy *92*
ServiceScape *98*
Skyword *101*
Toptal *105*
Upwork *108*
Workana *114*
Zirtual *118*
99designs *121*

Chapter 4: Steps to Success **126**
Statement of Work *128*
Writing a good job post *144*
Shortlisting candidates pre-interview *159*
Interview questions *165*
Shortlisting candidates post-interview *172*
Onboarding *174*
Creating training guides for your team *177*

Chapter 5: Frustrations of outsourcing **182**
Trust issues *183*
Poor quality work *187*
Missed deadlines *190*

2

    Disappearing freelancers *193*
    Slow responses *195*
    Half-finished projects *198*
    Team conflicts *199*
    Monitoring performance *202*
    Miscommunication *203*
    Language barriers *204*
    Low-context and high-context culture *205*
    NDAs and NCAs *207*
    Direct client interaction *210*
    Firing a freelancer *213*

Conclusion **216**

Appendix I: Outsourceable job categories **220**

Appendix II: Further freelance marketplaces **229**

Appendix III: Tools of the Trade **233**

Acknowledgements **251**

About the Author **252**

Preface

While hiring a freelancer isn't a new concept, it can be difficult for many people to understand why they would want to hire someone they may never physically meet. In reality, it's not hugely different from hiring someone to complete services in your home or business, say, for cleaning or gardening, or hiring an IT company to take care of your business network. The main difference is that your access to freelancers is worldwide and covers almost any specialism you can think of. In this digital era, the freelance market has expanded into online spaces that cover everything from writing, editing and graphic design through to personal assistance, data analysis, accounting, programming and much, much more.

What puts many people off this new way of working is the belief they need to see the person face to face, or they need to have the person complete the work sitting at a desk in their office. Yet the real focus should be on the outcome, not the means of how or where the work gets done.

Outsourcing to a freelancer is easier than you might think and allows you to get tasks and projects completed that you:

- hate to do
- don't have the skills to do
- don't have the time or inclination to do
- don't have the resources within your company to do

- shouldn't do as you should be focussing on what you're best at: growing your business, helping more people and making more money

As a business owner or entrepreneur, it's one of the best possible uses of your time and a superb investment when you get it right.

I've been outsourcing successfully for over a decade now, but I can't help think that if I had discovered it even sooner, my business would have grown even bigger and better, provided a greater range of services, helped more clients, and had an even stronger and happier core team, as they would have been solely focussed on what they were best at. Perhaps more importantly, if I'd learnt how to outsource earlier, I would have been given the greatest gift available in the business world: the gift of time.

In his novel *Animal Farm*, George Orwell famously wrote, 'All animals are equal, but some animals are more equal than others.' Orwell's novel delivered a broader comment on the inequalities present in wider society, yet the premise of his message can be applied to the way in which we experience time in the business world. Here, the number of hours we have is largely determined by the resources and staff at our disposal. This is why celebrities can put in a whopping six hours a day at the gym to look good for photoshoots, while the rest of us struggle to snatch thirty minutes!

Like everything from wealth distribution to health issues and more, life is not always fair in its distribution of time. While in theory we all have the same number of hours in our days, some have far less time *available* than others. Christina, a single mother of five that works two jobs during the week and another at the weekend, doesn't have the same twenty-four hours as Beyoncé or Colin Firth. To quote Benjamin Franklin, 'time is money,' and this is the primary reason that the rich continue to get richer and the poor, poorer. Just because you have a multi-million-dollar idea marinating in your head, doesn't mean you have the available time to turn it into a reality.

I first discovered this disparity of time distribution at the age of nineteen, when I was working my day job and simultaneously trying to start my own business. When it came to time allocation, I found myself in a constant tug of war. I knew I had to give my own business enough attention if I wanted it to become successful, but I still had to put in enough hours at my day job if I wanted to get paid. There was also the question of other commitments and maintaining a decent social life in between, and I came to the gradual understanding that if I wanted to translate my dreams into reality, I would have to find a way to make time work better for me. The million-selling author Stephen Covey mentions that the key is not in spending time, but in investing it, and I knew I had to find smarter ways to stretch whatever time I had available. With this idea in mind, I stumbled upon what is now known as outsourcing.

Outsourcing is an effective way of stretching the number of hours life has made available to you each day. By dividing up the jobs and responsibilities you have on your to-do list, you can increase efficiency and profit, and expand the limits of your business, all while having time left to devote to whatever is important to you.

The 21st century has seen a marked increase in the rate of outsourcing as well as the number of freelancers available for work. With the global incline in unemployment, there has been a surge of qualified individuals moving towards this novel market. For example, a 2019 report by CNBC demonstrates an increase in the freelance market with 57 million Americans currently enrolled for freelancing opportunities compared with 53 million people in 2014.

The Covid-19 pandemic brought about a swift upsurge in people working remotely. Organisations had to adapt quickly to set up their teams to work from home while also reaching out to the freelance marketplace for assistance. The freelance economy has and will continue to benefit greatly from this, and many companies that previously would have questioned home working, let alone outsourcing tasks or projects, now realise it can and does work. It's no longer about ensuring staff work the exact number of hours they are contracted for or employee visibility to justify salary; it's about the outcome. In many cases, it's about survival.

Whether you are on the supply or demand side, outsourcing represents a huge part of the future of work. Outsourcing is a win-win situation for the employer, the freelancer and their clients. While remote work is not a cure-all to make every person or business better, the benefits are numerous: less time spent commuting; fewer costs for staff members in travel, parking and lunches; less office space required; fewer vehicles on the road; more time with family and friends; fewer useless meetings; work completed while you sleep; access to great talent pools; no recruitment fees and reduced staffing costs; flexibility in staffing, allowing you to upscale and downscale when needed – the list goes on.

In *Outsourcing for Success*, I'll take you through all the benefits, drawbacks and processes of the various stages of outsourcing. I'll give you the lowdown on the best freelance marketplaces and pinpoint the best sites for specific types of talent and jobs/projects. I'll also give you the step-by-step guide on the system you need to have in place to make a success of your outsourcing journey. Along the way, I'll include two real-life case studies of entrepreneurs who have built their business using freelance talent including companies that have grown from $0 to $25m per year. Finally, I'll address the frustrations you'll face using this business model and how best to minimise potential issues or eliminate them entirely.

Best of all, it's only a small book that will take around three hours to read. You can highlight points for future reference, dip into specific sections that you need help with and refer back to it time and time again. Most of your questions will be answered organically as you progress through this book, but if they aren't, please feel free to reach out to me at kevashcroft.com and I'll do my best to help.

According to the American author and motivational speaker Eric Thomas, to change your life, you first have to change your twenty-four hours. Let me help you change your twenty-four hours by laying out the pros and cons of outsourcing and providing you with the steps to success in how to make the most of your time, energy and money.

Introduction

I grew up in the East End of Glasgow, Scotland, with my mother and four siblings. Although my father left before I was born, my mother did all she could despite poor health to take care of her children. A superstar of a woman who worked three jobs, she would get up and complete her first job while we slept. She would then wake us up and get us ready for the day ahead, before heading out to her second job. When we returned from school, she'd be there to make us dinner and then head out to her evening job before tucking us in to bed later that night.

I didn't enjoy school and struggled to find it engaging in any real way. It would be fair to say I didn't flourish in the environment of being taught 'at' and unsurprisingly, given that I'd bunked off the majority of my last two years, I left at the age of fifteen with no formal qualifications. I started my first job, which paid somewhere in the region of 70p per hour, and began training myself in technology, a personal interest of mine. By the time I was seventeen, my skills landed me a job that yielded £6,000 per year – what would I do with all this money, I thought? I soon found out just how quickly it would disappear after I passed my driving test and bought my first used car!

Irrespective of the other challenges I faced, I worked hard to up my game and when I was nineteen, I decided to start my own part-time business. I got off to a good start, winning a few new clients mainly from leafleting the local business area, and things were going from strength to strength. However, the opposite was true for the company that employed me for my full-time job. Their business had started to shrink.

As the old saying goes, 'You can't serve two masters,' and I vividly remember the day one of the directors approached me.

'Kev, you need to do your thing or our thing,' he said. 'You can't keep doing both.'

I loved my full-time job. It had grown significantly in responsibility and pay over the previous eighteen months and my colleagues were nice. Nevertheless, I realised instantly that while a decision-making moment was being forced on me, it presented an opportunity. After seven seconds of thought, I looked the director in the eye, thanked him for the ultimatum and confirmed I would be doing my own thing. And so, in November 1991, I opened my first office with a small brown desk and a telephone in the building of my previous employer.

I'm not one of those people who say they knew exactly what they wanted to be and the stars all aligned perfectly. The truth is, I was unsure of my every move. What I was sure of though, was that I was ready to learn. My first couple of months progressed at a slow pace, mainly because I sat on my bum and waited for the business to come to me. Strangely, in those first two months, I somehow put less effort into gaining new business than I ever would again. I've since realised that having a great idea and being good at what you do isn't enough. You need to plan, you need to be determined and committed, you need to follow through and continually move forward.

When I understood what was required, the business began to grow at a healthy rate. Not long after things had started to pick up, some of the staff from my previous employer came to work for me. I leveraged on this opportunity as they had years of experience and we already had an existing relationship. Everybody won: my previous employer was relieved of costs they were struggling to manage; the staff got a new job in the same building that suited them better; I got a ready-made team; and our clients benefited from great service.

When I discovered it was better to pay somebody to do the work that I didn't want or have time to do, I found I had time to focus on business strategies. With this increased strategic focus, I realised that my greatest strength was my ability to outsource and leverage the strength of others. It was a great success for everyone involved.

Few understand the concept and reasons behind outsourcing and of those already doing it; many are doing it the wrong way. For some, outsourcing is simply cheap labour. For me, outsourcing was primarily an efficiency strategy, i.e. how do I find the best people to help with this project, to get it done in the best possible way and with a focus on time for both me and my clients.

When I sold my IT company to a telecoms PLC in 2011, I decided that my next business would not have a team operating from a fixed location. It would be built as a distributed team of freelancers operating from their own locations, with their own equipment and their own self-employed mindset. It would be about the goal of the task or project, not about seeing a person arrive at 9.00 a.m. and leave at 5.00 p.m. Since embracing this mindset, I've engaged with thousands of freelancers, hired hundreds and spent high six-figure amounts on multiple freelancer platforms.

Although outsourcing has numerous benefits, like any other business strategy, it also has its risks. Communication gaps, unfinished projects and confidentiality breaches are just a few of the risks associated with outsourcing. It's worth noting that these issues also exist in a traditional business set-up. Over the years I've developed strategies to help mitigate these risks and I'll be sharing my wealth of experiences in this book, as well as guiding you through the process so you can jumpstart your foray into outsourcing or improve your experience of outsourcing so far.

Although some traditional businesses frown at the concept of outsourcing, it is my belief that this is because they don't fully understand it and are therefore perhaps fearful. When properly applied, outsourcing is proven to improve efficiency, encourage specialisation, speed up the slow, bureaucratic process of product and service development, and provide a pool of diverse talents from around the world.

It is important to recognise that outsourcing is not a fashionable move, it's a sensible move. With the lessons learned from Covid-19, it is even an essential move, not least to keep pace with your competitors and stay afloat.

There was a time when the only way to pass a message to someone in a distant country was via the post office. Just as the internet, and the telephone before it, made instant communication with people in distant countries a reality, it has changed the landscape with regards to outsourcing, vastly increasing its reach. As you flip through the pages of this book, I hope you will discover that outsourcing is not just a trend for a successful business to adapt and survive in the 21st century – it is a basic requirement for success and something that can make a positive impact on your life and business.

Despite the clear benefits to outsourcing, let us begin by examining the whole picture. Outsourcing isn't a one-size-fits-all solution – it needs to be applied skilfully, and with care and precision. In my first chapter I am going to discuss the many disadvantages as well as the advantages, to help you decide how you can best use outsourcing to boost your business model, while adjusting your expectations accordingly.

Chapter 1: Why outsource?

Outsourcing isn't simply about reducing operating costs. While some organisations may turn to outsourcing to trim the fat, having access to a larger pool of expertise or getting tasks and projects completed while you sleep may be the draw. Benefiting from the services of others as and when needed without entering into a long-term contract is a game changer for anyone's business.

Freelancing and the gig economy were popular even before outsourcing became popular, and the idea of hiring external consultants has been around for a long time. Mergers, business sales, legal matters, finance and IT are all some of the reasons organisations keep consultants on a retainer. Yet though similar, outsourcing is not the same as consulting. Consulting means getting an expert opinion, while outsourcing means getting expert work. While both can be combined, they are not mutually dependent. Freelancing as a form of outsourcing will be the focus of this book.

At the time of writing, it is estimated that there are approximately two million freelancers in the UK. A report from the Association of Independent Professionals and the Self Employed (IPSE) suggests the number of skilled freelancers has increased by 46% from 2008 to 2017, as published by the UK Freelance Industry Statistics. And why not? Freelancers get to do what they love and, in many cases, they can choose the hours they want and the people they want to work with. Since the outbreak and spread of the

Covid-19 pandemic, there has been a further increase in freelancing as a form of outsourcing on platforms like Upwork, Fiverr, PeoplePerHour and Toptal. With the rise in demand for remote working, today's businesses need to adapt to survive the current economic reality. Freelancing should be used as a strategic resource by organisations seeking flexibility and specific expertise.

One of your first questions might be simply, what kind of freelance talent is available? Sometimes it's hard to know where to start if you don't know which jobs can be undertaken remotely. For a full, comprehensive list of freelance talent courtesy of Upwork, please see Appendix I: Outsourceable Job Categories. There you'll find everything from professionals offering data entry, transcription and bookkeeping, to experts in solar energy, jewellery design and photography.

In my experience, outsourcing presents an exciting opportunity for businesses looking to upscale and take advantage of a unique business position or strategy. Equally, it makes it easier to downscale your business depending on client demands. Meanwhile, outsourcing also offers benefits to the freelancers, who can command their own rates, reduce or eliminate their commute, and gain more personal and family time. Let's examine those benefits – and some disadvantages – in more detail.

Benefits for business owners

Cost reduction

Let's imagine Bill owns a small IT start-up in the US and needs two full-time developers. Hiring local in-house developers would likely cost him somewhere in the region of $150,000 a year. This amount only increases if they are senior developers. However, if the work is outsourced to India or the Ukraine, he would expect to pay between $50,000 and $100,000 in total. This represents a saving of between $50,000 and $100,000 compared with the costs of hiring in-house staff, and is testament to the sometimes outrageous cost-saving potentials of outsourcing. The rates for India and Ukraine can be lower than this, but I've intentionally used these figures to demonstrate experienced freelancers with many positive reviews. Please note any figures I mention in this book are based in US dollars as that's the currency used by most of the freelance marketplaces.

Another area where savings can be made is in accommodation. As freelancers work from their own homes or offices, businesses don't need to foot the bill for setting up physical spaces for their employees. You no longer have to cover any rent or equipment costs; this is all paid for by the freelancer and the only cost to the business is for the services rendered.

One of the many beautiful things about outsourcing and freelancing is that they both operate under the gig economy and employees are paid per job/gig. They're not directly employed, meaning no pension contributions, no national insurance and no paid leave. Plus there's no need to employ someone full-time if you don't have a full-time role for them.

Think of outsourcing as a form of online shopping – but with talent. You can search through a large pool of qualified people at your own pace until you find the person that fits your requirements both in terms of finances and quality.

Unlike in traditional employment where the staff are often recruited based on sentiment and references, with outsourcing, your team is built based on referrals, expertise, qualifications and zeal to get the work done. Unique to online outsourcing is the evidence of the work they've completed in the past, in the form of portfolios, reviews and testimonials. Once a job is completed, if it's not to the client's expectations, payment can be withheld. This provides a strong motivation for the freelancer to get the job done on time and to a high standard. In addition, poor reviews can lead to less work in the future, and these two factors alone are reasons why freelancers make some of the most dedicated and motivated employees possible. To avoid misuse of the system, most freelancing sites have rules in place that not only protect the client and their money when the freelancer doesn't deliver, but also protects the freelancer and their integrity in cases where the client is being obstinate and troublesome.

All things being equal, accomplished and experienced freelancers that have a proven track record but also happen to be on the more expensive side will likely do a fantastic job. However, some freelancers that have much lower rates can also do just as well. Like every employment circle, freelancing has tiers and ladders to be climbed and there are numerous talented but unknown freelancers who, in a bid to get more reviews and visibility on the platform, offer excellent services at unbelievable prices. A conscientious outsourcer on a budget will do well to seek out these diamonds in the rough.

Businesses on a budget are more likely to be able to afford a more experienced and skilled part-time person, as there's no obligation to hire them full time. No traditional recruitment costs and no ongoing commitment make this an attractive proposition.

Risk reduction

From time immemorial, one of the mantras in business and economic circles is the interconnectedness of business and risk. With outsourcing, risk stops being endemic to business.

The contract between the outsourcer and the freelancer is a unique agreement quite unlike anything between an employer and his physical employees. The contract is subject to renewal and can be terminated if the services of the freelancer are no longer satisfactory or needed, as opposed to traditional contract agreements where the employer just has to deal with the excesses of their employees.

The benefits of outsourcing become even more apparent when working with an agency. Different members can be cycled in and out of the outsourcer's organisation until a perfect match is found, and if at any time that perfect match stops being so perfect or the services of the freelance agency become subpar, the outsourcer can move on to another agency entirely.

With outsourcing, the chances of losing money when investing or sourcing human capital are greatly reduced so long as the correct processes and procedures are followed. In a classic case of having your cake and eating it, the outsourcer's funds can even be returned if the service rendered doesn't meet expectations or in any way deviates from the terms of the agreement.

Should your business expand or shrink, it is far simpler to upscale or downscale with this business model as your clients and the economy dictates.

Wealth of expertise

With traditional hiring, what you see is rarely what you get. I've said for decades that people come for an audition rather than an interview. The audition goes well, you get a good feeling, and their cherry-picked references are, of course, faultless. However, you don't really know what you're getting until the employee is a part of your team and working alongside others. By that point, you've already invested a large amount of time and money in them.

Thanks to reviews, with outsourcing you are in a far greater position of certainty that what you see is what you will get. Over and above basic star or percentage ratings, you can read client testimonials and discover what clicked for them, along with what didn't work. You can also see how the freelancer has dealt with the feedback, which should help you further decide if this is likely to be a good fit for you.

The larger sites showcase a vast number of people from all around the world to pick from, each bringing a new flavour and outlook with their own unique experiences. Often, this mishmash of competencies and creativity can be just the 'it' factor your business needs.

Essentially, outsourcing increases a firm's access to multiple streams of information, ideas, and input, all at a fair price. Imagine marketing content is needed for a new product. A firm can engage two or three freelancers for as little as $50 each to develop a social media advert representing the product. The freelancers will develop different content based on their experience, background, expertise and personal beliefs, which grants a business owner options and more possibilities. The benefit of organising small tasks like the above to test the skills and the fit of the people *before* you add them to your team is invaluable, and cannot be underestimated.

Outsourcing allows you to tap into the skills of a specialist for specific tasks they are great at and can do in a reasonable timeframe, whether that be social media graphics, a financial report, a presentation, or adding new features to your website, the list is endless. Well, not quite endless, but for a comprehensive idea of which tasks can be outsourced, please see Appendix I: Outsourceable Job Categories.

More time to focus on core competencies

Through its inherent limitedness and non-renewability, time is our most valuable resource. The success of any business, small or large, start-up or established, depends on the amount of time key players devote to strategic activities. This is what separates a successful business from its less successful counterparts. Amazon would not be the giant it is right now if Jeff Bezos was stuck juggling company advertisements, customer relations, feedback, and designing for the site.

As a business owner, you cannot take your business to the heights you envision if you spend your time focusing on every task. This may be required and possible when the business is still in its infancy, but there comes a point when this becomes unsustainable and recruiting outside help becomes indispensable. Making use of outsourcing frees up your time, which in turn will help ease stress and enable you to focus on more important tasks, such as generating new ideas and content, and connecting more with your potential customers/clients.

Another aspect that fits with this is the potential outsourcing has for shifting business owners from the 'I -

must-do-it-all mindset' to the 'task delegation' mindset. When you first start a business, it is normal and even expected that you may become slightly neurotic. You have tons of ideas in your head and a decent plan of how to achieve them, yet others cannot see those ideas as clearly. Many business owners become a jack of all trades and, unsurprisingly, a master of none. If you're reading this and thinking, 'I've done this for ten years and my business is better off for it,' you might well be wrong. By effectively utilising outsourcing, your businesses would likely be doing much better than it already is, as you'd have had more time to focus on growth. Just because you *can* do something, doesn't mean you *should*. It is progressively underproductive both to yourself and your business to try and do everything yourself.

Flexible staffing and huge talent pool

Outsourcing offers firms a number of benefits over traditional employment methods with respect to staffing. Rather than employing a team of staff directly and dealing with all the associated ups and downs, outsourcing allows much more flexibility. With direct employees, if a member of the team moves on or retires, the expensive and sometimes lengthy process of replacing them must start again. Likewise, if you need to fire someone or make them redundant, this can be stressful, upsetting, costly and a time-consuming exercise. The new employee then needs time to gel with the rest of the team and settle down – and this really is the best-case scenario! Meanwhile, if a freelancer chooses not to continue working with you, provides subpar work or behaves in an unacceptable manner, replacing them is a much faster and simpler task than terminating the contract of a direct employee.

Moreover, outsourcing staff allows a firm to widen its potential by having a much larger number of workers at their disposal compared with more traditional employment methods. With no hint of exaggeration, a firm could have their pick of millions of freelancers, each with different specialities, qualifications and experience levels. They could then be called upon at short notice to begin working on a project, irrespective of their physical location. Compare this with managing a small number of direct employees juggling their time between projects and often working on tasks outside their skill set and comfort zone.

While employing an expert rather than a generalist may cost more per hour, the quality of the work completed will be better and the timescale from start to finish is often far shorter. This in turn helps you get paid faster and provides a great client experience, which will hopefully have them coming back for more as well as recommending you to others.

For example, if I need a person to complete some Google Tag Manager configuration and optimisation, I don't need to train an existing member of the team in that skill set, nor do I need to hire an agency to complete a specific project for me and all that entails. I can outsource the work to an experienced freelancer who specialises in that field and who can get it right first time, on time and for a competitive price.

One of the best parts of outsourcing for me is finishing my day and passing the next stage of work over to people in my team to complete during my downtime and while I'm asleep. There's nothing quite as satisfying as waking up to work already completed that I can push straight to my client for comment.

Location advantages

Thanks to the internet, borders are blurring as the world shrinks into what is often called a 'global village'. In conjunction with the much larger pool of expertise, there's really no geographical limit when it comes to outsourcing. An organisation can find specialists in almost any location without leaving the comfort of their armchair and without having a physical presence in that country. With traditional practices, a firm looking to hire a tech specialist in India would have to visit the country and do the necessary time-consuming and expensive legwork. When everything such as flights, accommodation and expenses are considered, the cost might be just too high for the endeavour to be cost effective.

If you require a presence in a local area, a native to speak to clients or suppliers, or someone to serve a specific time zone, outsourcing makes it easy and may help you win and retain customers and contracts, allowing you to expand into different countries around the world with far greater ease.

Benefits for freelancers

While this book focuses on outsourcing from the business owner's perspective, I'm including details of the benefits to the freelancers you will work with, as this new economy really is a win-win for everyone involved. Equally, freelancers approach work with a different mindset to their traditionally employed counterparts, and it is useful to familiarise yourself with their motivations and rationale.

Working at their convenience

Few people enjoy a 6.00 a.m. alarm or the congested roads, trains, and buses that follow, as you battle to make it into the office. Once you finally arrive, no one wants to deal with cut-throat co-workers vying for attention or a draconian boss looking to sap as much from you as possible in the hours you're there. Office politics and power struggles are not what makes the world go round for most of us. What if you were told that all of these niggles could be a thing of the past?

Freelancing offers a viable solution to all of these mini dramas while maintaining the challenging atmosphere that's needed for growth and development. Employment can be so much easier and far less stress inducing.

We all have different times throughout the day when we are most productive. While some people can and do give their best during the traditional working hours of nine to five, others operate best at 6.00 a.m. Others still find their creativity peaks in the middle of the night, and there's nothing wrong with that. As Aristotle once said, 'No great mind ever existed without some touch of madness,' and we all have weird rituals and quirks that help us get work done. It's what makes us human. The success of accepting these quirks can be seen in the untraditional office spaces created by companies like Google, that feature bright colours and video games surrounded by sofas and hammocks. If a wildly successful business such as Google can accept that the mould needs to be broken, perhaps it's time more did too. Without the expense of an extravagant office space, outsourcing allows freelancers the ability to work at their convenience. Everything is acceptable – working at the park or the café, at 2.00 a.m. in pyjamas or at a desk wearing a suit and tie. Flexibility and choice are two of the many things that make freelancing so appealing.

Although skilled freelancers may not get job promotions and other benefits that come with traditional employers, they frequently earn more than 70% of other workers in the US with little to no stress. Furthermore, approximately 51% of them reportedly believe they would struggle to return to the traditional job setting, claiming it to be boring, restrictive and with very low returns.

High pay-out

There's something especially gratifying about getting paid for work you enjoy and that's done at your own convenience. With traditional employment, you sometimes have to stomach unfavourable conditions to the point that your salary seems paltry compared to the stress you endure. Freelancers, on average, are less stressed and earn sometimes twice what the average employee would receive in traditional employment settings. For example, an editor attached to a physical company can expect to earn somewhere in the region of $50,000 per year, whereas freelance editors using platforms such as Upwork, Reedsy and Livingstone can earn over $70,000. Of course, the traditional employee may receive added benefits within that salary such as pensions, gym memberships and health insurance, not applicable within the freelance world.

Positive instant gratification

Freelancing, and indeed the gig economy, operates on what I like to call positive instant gratification. Freelancing is an earn-as-you-work arrangement. Unlike traditional employment where you have to wait for payday once a month, with freelancing, payment is received shortly after work is submitted. Instant gratification gets a bad rap, especially in this era of mindfulness and awareness, however, it can often spur us on to be more, do more and accomplish more. Getting paid instantly (or within a couple of weeks on some marketplaces) gives an immediate sense of achievement along with a physical release of dopamine. With more work equalling more pay and another release of dopamine, freelancers are understandably some of the most driven and efficient workers in the world of employment.

Larger pool of clients

Using online marketplaces exposes freelancers to thousands more job opportunities on a marketplace than they would be in the outside world, where they might be limited by location, lack of experience or referrals. As they work their way up the ladder, attracting positive reviews, their profiles are raised, allowing them to be matched or showcased to potential clients they would never have encountered otherwise.

There's an almost endless supply of opportunities for freelancers and just as businesses are not limited to a single country, freelancers can search for and accept jobs from around the world provided they have the necessary skills. Geographical location becomes a non-issue and allows people from traditionally poorer countries to earn far more than the average salary in their region.

Little or no set-up cost

As most jobs can be completed from the comfort of your home, there's no need to set up or hire an office or workspace, and equally you can save on travel-associated costs, commuting time and stress. All that's needed is a computer, a telephone and a reliable internet connection, which are all things most of us already have.

An attractive side hustle

The coronavirus pandemic has shown us all just how fragile our lives can be, not only in terms of health but in terms of finances and employment. It's shown us that having multiple streams of income can provide a much-needed financial cushion to fall back on should the worst happen.

Many day jobs offer little room for growth and financial freedom, and are characterised by job insecurity. Despite this, they are still the reality for the vast majority of people and this is unlikely to change in the near future. If you are someone that wants to maintain a traditional nine-to-five, freelancing could still be an attractive proposition as a 'side hustle'. Flexible hours are the main draw for people in this position and work can be made to fit in around your current schedule. So long as it is given adequate time and planning, freelancing is a viable option to combine with more traditional employment to provide a second income stream and offer enhanced financial security.

Option to become an agency

A common yet little-known practice among freelancers is something that can be referred to as micro-outsourcing. Micro-outsourcing is where a more experienced and successful freelancer will take on more work than they can complete and then outsource it, either partially or in its entirety, to other freelancers working at far lower rates than the client is paying the experienced freelancer. When the work is finished, the experienced freelancer checks it over and polishes it up where necessary, then gives it his signature before handing it over to the client. In this manner, a freelancer can become an employer in his own right. With the time, growth and experience gained on the job, he can become something of an expert in their field. Of course, this step up in experience can command higher rates of pay, and by employing a small team and coaching them to improve, higher rates of pay combined with the possibility of completing a greater workload means a far greater income.

Not only is this something that works well for suitable freelancers, it is a way for anyone to build a new business without the need for the budget required to set up a traditional business. For example, a skilled IT project manager who knows their clients' businesses inside out could quite easily start their own remote IT firm fully staffed with an experienced and skilled team from around the world and deliver all the services necessary.

Client selectivity

In traditional employment settings, you have little to no say over which clients you do or do not work with. Your boss calls the shots and you act accordingly. With freelancing, however, you are the boss and you make the decisions on who you want to work with. There's no superior to strongarm you into doing jobs you're not interested in, and you can't be reprimanded for rejecting work. If a client seems like too much stress, or there's a personality clash, or their work is dull or out of your area of expertise, you can simply refuse the job at your discretion.

Pursuing passion projects

Being good at something and being passionate about it are two separate concepts that are often confused in the employment world. Few people understand that it is possible to be good at something without being passionate about it. Conversely, it is rare to be passionate about something without being good at it, as passion often drives interest and hard work. As opposed to traditional employment, freelancing is quality-centric rather than quantity-centric. In an extension of the previous point, not only do you get to select clients, you get to select individual jobs and projects you are passionate about. As a freelance writer, for example, you could choose to focus on science fiction novels, rather than simply accepting every commission that comes your way, regardless of genre.

Disadvantages for business owners

Like most things in life, outsourcing is not devoid of risks and downsides, and it is these risks that make many people wary about venturing into the world of outsourcing.

Costs

The cost-effective nature of outsourcing has already been covered, but, like all things in business, outsourcing can potentially be costly to a firm if effective planning and efficient outsourcing strategies are not applied. Many clients and organisations get excited at the prospect of outsourcing and jump in head first. They approach the freelancer with the best reviews and the highest prices, thinking that guarantees a good job, or conversely they opt for the lowest-cost freelancer and don't put in the effort with a proper Statement of Work (SOW), onboarding or training. This leads to poor quality work, delays and costs in time and money.

Security

Online work necessitates the need for security and privacy to be considered so as to provide protection for sensitive data. Bribery, corruption and cybersecurity are critical issues in the modern corporate landscape, and there is potential for freelancers to reproduce a particular work or leak sensitive details about a job to another party, just like in a traditional business set-up. It is therefore important to have these factors under careful consideration when choosing a freelancer for your project. For particularly sensitive work, it is always recommended that freelancers are asked to sign legal documents, such as a non-disclosure agreement (NDA), to protect the content involved. If the terms of the contract are breached in any way, the client can opt either for monetary or injunctive relief.

Communication and logistics

To paraphrase Cameron Herold, author of *Meetings Suck* and founder of the COO Alliance, communication is essential to success in the business world. Effective communication is what makes your organisation, and all its parts, function like a well-oiled machine. When there is a breakdown in communication, every part of the organisation has the potential to breakdown. Communication is as much physical as it is verbal and textual, and body language can play a huge role in effectively communicating our wishes and desires.

Communication can be one aspect of outsourcing that suffers for a variety of reasons. Sometimes it is nothing more than because you are working across a physical divide, while other times things are lost in translation. When dealing with freelancers in foreign countries, it can be problematic when both parties do not speak the same language and while this can be curbed somewhat through video conferencing such as Zoom and Skype, a language barrier is not ideal. That's not to say the business relationship is a non-starter, simply that it is important to establish good communication, however that may be. Of course, good communications isn't always about vocabulary: it's important to establish an understanding and a connection between client and freelancer.

Another common problem with freelancing is the issue of logistics. Some of the best freelancers often live in different time zones and can sometimes have problems accessing a reliable internet connection. While conflicting time zones can be managed by adjusting deadlines, poor connectivity can present real problems. Inability to connect to the internet may cause a freelancer to miss a deadline and can inhibit good communication. If as a client you are aware that the freelancer you are considering is in a country or region where connectivity might be an issue, speak with them and raise your concerns. Ask about the speed and reliability of their internet connection and the reliability of their power supply.

Disadvantages for freelancers

The elusive work-life balance

The convenience and flexibility freelancing brings is not without consequences and the line between work and home life can often become blurred, causing the freelancer to work more and give less time to life's other activities. This scenario is detrimental to the freelancer and the quality of work they produce, so it is important to follow a few simple steps to create a fair balance between work and leisure. Creating a plan for the day and setting out a clear workstation are among the good habits that can prevent the freelancer from overworking.

Unpredictable work and cash flow

Despite its numerous advantages, instability and unpredictability are some of the dominant features of the gig economy. While sometimes a freelancer can be flooded with work and every day is a pay day, unfortunately, dry spells where jobs are few and far between can be a sad reality. In a traditional employment setting, all of the risks are borne by the employer and the steady pay cheque, regardless of workflow, is a real comfort. Due to freelancing's nature of earn-as-you-work, some months may be thin on the work front, meaning your income will take a hit, and it is this inconsistency that forces freelancers to live from job to job. As a result, gaining the financial freedom that most of us strive for becomes difficult.

Micro-outsourcing gone wrong

Micro-outsourcing is one of the tools that freelancers can use to do multiple jobs with little to no effort. In a situation where micro-outsourcing goes as planned, the client's job is completed satisfactorily and the freelancer gets paid. Both parties are happy. However, things can and do go wrong with micro-outsourcing. There is always the possibility of the second freelancer doing a bad job, or worse, not delivering at all. The responsibility then falls back to the freelancer that took the job to either undertake a large workload in a short space of time, or make it known to the client that the deadline will be missed. Both scenarios can have financial implications for both parties. In extreme cases, the second freelancer could leak or reproduce sensitive elements, thus affecting the integrity and reputation of the original freelancer.

Multiple bosses

Many people enter into the world of freelancing with the draw that they will get to be their own boss. While this may be technically true, there are obligations to clients that need to be met and complete autonomy does not exist. If a freelancer chooses to undertake multiple jobs at a time, this can lead to them having to answer to many people simultaneously, feeling just like they might in a traditional workplace setting.

No benefits

Despite the unappealing image nine-to-five jobs have among younger generations, it's difficult to deny the benefits many of these jobs come with. From maternity and paternity pay, paid annual leave, paid sick leave and pensions, to extras such as company cars and bonuses, traditional employment certainly comes with a complete package. Freelancing, on the other hand, is all about you. If you're sick and can't work, you don't get paid. Similarly, if you want a holiday, you don't get paid. Everything is down to the individual and it's entirely your responsibility to plan for all eventualities.

Lack of structure

In today's world, it's easy to see the traditional workplace as the big bad wolf that frustrates growth and freedom, stifles creativity, and makes the rat race the very centre of your existence. However, working a nine-to-five also has its benefits, one of which is being a set structure. Freedom, while exhilarating and potentially wonderful for creativity, can leave you feeling unfocused and confused. Paired with a sometimes questionable work-life balance, this lack of structure can trigger low levels of productivity and limit growth. To combat this, setting out a plan (and sticking to it) can help to add structure to your day. Microsoft Windows has a built-in feature called Focus that limits notifications, while multiple apps are available for MacOS. Use them. Avoid checking your social media while you're working, keep your phone out of sight and stick to the roster of work you have on your plate.

Managing expectations

Many people new to outsourcing have a number of expectations that turn out to be different from what they experience, so having an idea of what to expect is useful to avoid disappointment. The most common concerns I hear are:

- How can I be sure they will do the work if I can't see them?
- How can I trust someone if I've not met them in person?
- Will I get ripped off?
- It's just cheap labour, which makes me feel uncomfortable
- I don't want to send work to other countries
- The quality of work will be poor
- It's too much hassle

Firstly, I urge you not to focus on the old-fashioned school of thought that an employee needs to be seen to ensure they are working to their full potential. Secondly, you need to embrace the mindset that outsourcing is all about the results and that's what you pay for. If you don't get the results, you don't make a payment. It's as simple as that.

Just as you can be ripped off by a member of staff in a traditional set-up, you can befall the same fate dealing with remote freelancers. The key here is to have strong processes and procedures in place as well as adequate security for whatever tasks or projects are being carried out. Allow access to what people need and nothing more.

My advice is to think of freelancers more as self-employed people rather than part-time or full-time employees. If they don't work, they don't get paid. If they don't do a good job, they get a bad review and potentially don't get paid. There are exceptions to the rule, but all of this generally leads to a situation where the freelancers are keen to do a great job, get a great review and to continue to work with you and others to improve their ratings, rates and quality of life.

While it's true you can hire people at what seems like ridiculously low rates, the majority of freelancers earn more as freelancers than they would as employees. On platforms like Upwork and others you'll see hourly rates from $3 per hour to hundreds of dollars per hour. You'll also see fixed price contracts from $10 through to tens of thousands.

While it's a fact that many freelancers initially start with low rates to gain a presence on a new platform, some freelancers have low rates simply because they do not offer a high level of service. As a client, you might not always be looking for the very best and might be willing to settle for something that's a little rough around the edges to save a bit of money. The point is to keep your expectations in line with reality and not to expect high quality work for nominal prices. With that said, it's worth remembering that a freelancer offering services for $5 or $6 an hour isn't necessarily low skilled, and that amount could be well above the cost of living in the country they work from. Perhaps they're offering top-notch work at lower prices than other freelancers simply because it represents a great rate where they live.

The quality of work you receive is directly affected by how well you set out your task/project requirements, how proficient a job post you write to attract potential candidates, your shortlisting and interview skills, and your final onboarding and agreement with the freelancer or agency. Bear in mind that every marketplace you work with will have some form of review and rating system for the freelancers in place, which you can use to research your freelancer, but also report on any problematic or unexpected experiences.

Finally, it's important that you're ready and willing to accept the possibility that a freelancer may not be able to deliver on their promise. There can be many reasons for this, including the freelancer realising they are out of their depth, illness or the offer of a better contract elsewhere. This is no different to the potential pitfalls of working with a traditional employee, so you need to have a contingency plan in place in case this happens.

I can tell you from my own personal experience of operating with a virtual team and employing hundreds over the last ten years, the number of issues I've had is small, and because I've always had a fallback plan in place, the disturbances to the business have been minimal.

A fallback plan doesn't need to be hugely detailed. It can be as simple as maintaining a relationship with other freelancers who can step in at short notice. It can be including contingencies into your project to allow for changing timescales and also budget in case you need to hire a more expensive freelancer with more experience.

Chapter 2: Case Studies

FreeUp

FreeUp, which will also be one of the featured marketplaces in the next chapter, is a great example of a company that has grown via a strategy to build the majority of the team as freelancers rather than the traditional direct employment method. Founded at the end of 2015 by Nathan Hirsch and Connor Gillivan with a $5,000 investment, it was envisaged as a way to recruit freelancers who could help them expand their existing Amazon business. At its peak, FreeUp managed over half a million products on their store, selling over $25 million of goods on the e-commerce marketplace.

As Nathan and Connor built their own business using freelancers, they realised there was an opportunity to help connect the best freelancers with other clients who required similar services. They pushed on from the original Amazon focus and started to offer freelancers in other niches like marketing, virtual assistance, graphic design, video editing and more.

From their initial $5,000 investment, FreeUp grew to $1 million, to $5 million, to $9 million and eventually $12 million dollars: fantastic growth over a five-year period.

In an interesting turn of events, it was one of their clients, The HOTH, who reached out to them and said, 'Hey, we love FreeUp. We've used FreeUp for a while. We want to get into the freelancer space, and we don't want to build it from scratch. Would you guys be interested in selling?'

After six months of due diligence, FreeUp was sold to The HOTH in late 2019. In a further twist, Nathan and Connor's new business is now a client of FreeUp and uses the same freelancers they used to hire out to others.

Matt Harrison, VP of Strategy at FreeUp, says, 'Without the use of freelancers in our core team, we would most certainly be at least two years behind where we are now. Specifically, our development team has come from years of trial and error with different developers. The same goes for the higher-end freelancers we've hired at different stages of the business to assist higher-end strategy. If we had abandoned the freelancer model with FreeUp, I believe we would not have coped with the reality of Covid as well as we have. Being nimble and with such a great depth and breadth of knowledge of the global landscape allowed us to find clients in many different regions.'

As of the end of December 2020, FreeUp has forty-two freelancers within their immediate group and five traditional employees who manage an average of 17,500 weekly billed hours through an average of 760 active freelancers and an average of 970 active clients each week.

Their Freelancer Success Team consists of eleven team members who manage an average of 2,350 freelancer applications each month. From these applications they select an average of 460 each month for video interviews, with the aim of allowing only 1% of applicants onto the FreeUp marketplace.

Since The HOTH acquired FreeUp, they have only had a staff turnover of three team members. More members of the FreeUp team have started working with other Next Net Media properties (the group that owns The HOTH and FreeUp). That's the beauty of having pre-vetted freelancers to work with – they were able to pick up other parts of the business and even help some of their other departments to make themselves more scalable.

While I'm not privy to the sale price, Nathan mentioned in an interview with Jaime Masters of *Eventual Millionaire* that they gave $500,000 to their team in the Philippines from the proceeds of the sale as a gift. This gives a small insight to the actual figure they must have achieved.

FreeUp is an excellent example of a business that has been scaled quickly and sold within a short space of time and that would have been far more difficult, more expensive and less likely to succeed if they had used traditional staffing methods.

The JAR Group

A.J. Lawrence sold his digital agency, The JAR Group, to investors including a private equity firm, a client and an employee, before exiting the company back in 2014. He retained the agency name and analytics, offering to start the next chapter of the business in his inimitable entrepreneurial way and as an investor and advisor in 2015.

The new business model focused on generating a base level of consistent revenue to allow A.J. to explore new ideas and business experiments, creating a more flexible environment to test different concepts more rapidly. As long as the experiments were interesting and added value, he looked to take them through a trial process to establish scalability.

This process included funnel building, affiliate development, buying and selling existing websites, and recently purchasing a highly respected and popular podcast, Beyond 8 Figures (https://Beyond8Figures.com).

As A.J. embarked on this new journey, he made a distinct decision not to hire any traditional full-time staff. He started his team using Upwork, Fiverr and select other online marketplaces. As his projects grew, he expanded to having a large group of predominantly dedicated freelancers, as A.J. calls it, 'to help run and build crazy projects.'

A.J.'s use of freelancers was never to source low-cost talent or save money. It was more to avoid taking on a large commitment. If an experiment or a project wasn't working out, he didn't want to be beholden from a team perspective.

While he didn't want to be beholden to a team, he wanted to ensure that those he did hire felt valued. So, whether they provide just a few hours or forty hours per week, they could contribute and grow individually and as a team.

Without having chosen the freelancing route, A.J. believes that many of his experiments and projects simply wouldn't have happened, and he would have missed out on some of the more exciting and profitable creations over the last few years. Using freelancers reduces his risk, increases his flexibility, and allows him to play around a little more with what's available – not something he would have done had he not taken advantage of the freelancer model.

A team of twelve freelancers provides a mix of hours from a few per week to forty-plus to help A.J. regularly. He's assembled a strong collection of individuals from many countries and cultures around the world. Having built his businesses using this model resulted in the Covid-19 pandemic having virtually no impact other than less travel and fewer face-to-face meetings.

The JAR Group holding company had a turnover of $1.4 million in 2020 and is on target to achieve approximately $2 million in 2021. Several projects are in a position where they are ready to scale and reach even higher figures for A.J. and his holdings.

Chapter 3: Freelance Marketplaces A-Z

Congratulations! You've decided to outsource. So where should you look for all this lovely talent you've been reading about so far? The good news is that there are many, many options out there and that's only likely to increase as time progresses. Thanks to the immediacy of the internet, finding your outsourced team is easier than ever before.

Once you've decided what kind of freelance talent you need, there is a multitude of marketplaces and platforms you can join and search to find your next team member or your entire team. However, these marketplaces are not all equal and often operate in different ways. Some charge the freelancer when they get paid, while others charge the client a membership fee and a fee for every job post they make and every person they hire. Some charge a fee based on the value of the hire. Some allow you to post jobs or competitions. Some sites even make you select from pre-made gigs.

It's important to research the various options to find the best fit for you, how you work and the type of freelancer or team you need to hire.

In this chapter, I've listed what I consider to be the Top Twenty outsourcing sites in terms of offering both general and niche service providers. There are, of course, many more sites available, and I have included a comprehensive list of these in Appendix II: Further Freelance Marketplaces.

Some of the better-known marketplaces include Upwork, Freelancer and Fiverr. They provide access to a wide range of professionals from accountants to designers, audio production to data mining, intellectual property to 3D modelling. Other marketplaces are much more specific in what they offer, for example, Design Pickle specialises in graphic design, while Reedsy specialises in publishing. They all have their own ways of working and they all have their own pros and cons that you need to understand and decide which one or ones are best for you.

Once you have selected your freelancers, you typically have the option of hiring them on an hourly rate, as you might a traditional employee, or you can hire them based on a fixed rate per job. There is no right or wrong way here; it's simply down to how you like to work and what makes more sense for you and your business.

Fixed-rate jobs provide both clients and freelancers with the peace of mind that the job spec is clarified upfront and it will be completed for an agreed amount (unless you change the goalposts, in which case you should obviously expect to pay more). Once the fee has been agreed, you typically transfer money into an escrow account so the freelancer knows you have the funds to pay for the contract, and work begins. Payment won't be released until you are happy specific milestones have been completed, or that the contract has been completed to your satisfaction.

As you would expect, freelance marketplaces can come and go. Some merge with others and new contenders appear as time goes on. Check out kevashcroft.com to keep up to date with the latest marketplaces and how they are performing for clients and freelancers.

CloudPeeps

Best for admin (virtual assistance), content writing, copywriting, design, development, marketing and SEO.
CloudPeeps is a growing freelance marketplace, founded in 2015, and has more than 20,000 customers. On this site, employers are referred to as clients and freelancers as peeps.

For clients, finding services, posting jobs and hiring is free. There are no service fees and no hidden fees. The only fee you pay is $150 to promote a job or purchase a concierge service, which is optional. After you sign up as a client, you need to set up your company profile and include details such as your website, where your company is located, company logo, number of team members, your field of business and links to your social profiles. You have the option to add users to access your company account on CloudPeeps so they too can post jobs, hire peeps, review invoices and so on.

You can search peeps using filters such as skill set, rate and time zone. Freelancers' profiles include the services packages they offer, their CloudPeeps clients, work history, reviews and past references. You can also view their portfolio projects, education level, skills, preferred tools, their availability and interests. You have four options to hire peeps on CloudPeeps. You can post jobs, purchase their service packages, you can click the Hire button to send a direct offer for work or you can message them to send your custom requests.

When you connect with a peep, you need to set up your job and job agreement directly on CloudPeeps. You can view all of your ongoing jobs and agreements on Manage Jobs on the dashboard. You also have the option to edit your job details and agreement with your peep at any time. On the CloudPeeps Rates page, you will find some sample freelance rates for both hourly and fixed-price projects. The fixed-price projects are priced per month or as a one-time charge. The hourly rate guide seems to show talent at the higher end of the scale rather than you'll find when you actually search their system.

The CloudPeeps platform allows clients to not only find new freelance talent, but also manage existing freelancer relationships and jobs, known as 'external' jobs. External job positions are charged a 1% service fee in conjunction with Stripe's standard transaction fees of 2.9% + $0.30. When you select a peep to hire on CloudPeeps, you will be charged $50, which gets credited towards your next invoice. Payment occurs via credit or debit card.

No freelance solution is foolproof, and like most marketplaces, CloudPeeps features a dispute resolution system. For hourly projects, when an invoice is manually submitted, you will need to raise any queries directly on the invoice during the Dispute Period, which is the review period after your peep sends you the invoice. This will pause the payment and allow you to take time and talk to your peep about the situation. In the case of fixed-price projects, you will be charged up front for your peep's work and the payment processes only after thirty days. If there's a dispute, you may pause or end the job or ask for a refund. Remember that payments that are released to the peep are non-refundable.

CloudPeeps is a small platform in comparison to the giants like Upwork and Fiverr. For example, if you search for designers around the world, you'll be presented with approximately 150 peeps to choose from at the time of writing. However, it is a growing community. At the time of writing, I noticed there were many improvements necessary on this platform. They have a private messaging system in place but there are no time tracking, work diary or reporting tools available, nor are there mobile applications. The UI of the desktop site is basic and usable, but there's room for improvement in the design aspects as well. Customer support appears reasonable, offering email support and callback requests.

Unusually, some of the people who have been involved in the founding and running of the company are actually available to hire on their own system.

Ratings:

- Glassdoor: 4.3 stars out of 5 based on 12 reviews
- Facebook: 4.0 stars out of 5 based on the opinions of 6 people

Highlights:

- Managing existing freelancer relationships
- Free to sign up and use
- Four ways to hire: posting jobs, purchasing service packages, sending direct offers or personal messages

Codeable

Best for designers and developers, digital marketers, content publishers and creatives.

Codeable is a group of freelance experts who specialise in WordPress. Founded in 2012, Codeable currently has more than 510 experts, 630+ partners, over 19,000 customers, and has more than 75,000 completed projects. Developers hail from more than sixty countries with the top represented locations being the United States, Canada, the United Kingdom, Romania, and Croatia. Ninety-seven per cent of Codeable experts have more than six years of professional WordPress experience. More than 2,000 projects are delivered every month by Codeable experts.

When you use Codeable to find developers, you get access to a pool of WordPress experts who have passed a rigorous hiring process. Out of thousands of applications, only 2% of applicants join the Codeable team. From small business owners, e-commerce store owners, and enterprise organisations to individuals and solopreneurs, anyone can hire developers using Codeable. From small tasks and fixes through website maintenance, migration, theme and plugin updates, security and speed optimisation and website customisation, you can have any of your WordPress-related tasks solved.

The vetting process starts with a comprehensive online application where the developer's English skills and professional WordPress experience are reviewed. In the second step, their technical knowledge, problem-solving abilities, and code quality are checked through a trial development task. Then, with a live interview and coding test, their personality, community skills, and technical abilities are evaluated in the third step. The fourth step requires them to pass The Codeable Academy exam: a course designed to verify familiarity with all of Codeable's operational rules and quality standards. Then, as a fifth step, they go through a forty-five-day trial period, after which they join the Codeable team. The sixth step is defined as ongoing excellence monitoring, where low-performing experts are removed quickly and with dignity.

If you know what you need, you can simply submit a project. If you need help in deciding your requirements, you can request a consultation with an expert, charged at $59 for one hour. Hiring on Codeable works in a three-step process. First you send your brief, then you are connected to the right developers to chat with, and in the third and final step, collaboration begins. After you submit your project, you are matched with a dedicated WordPress developer within one business day.

In the first step, you tell Codeable what you need in your brief. It can be anything from small bug fixes to large e-commerce websites. Secondly, you are connected with between one and five top experts with a shared workroom for accurate scoping of your project. Thanks to Codeable's internal matchmaking system, you will be connected with the most appropriate developers based on your requirements, their skill sets and availability. Unlike many other marketplaces, you don't search for the freelancer: a suitable selection is presented to you.

You can view the profiles of the experts who bid on your project or with whom you are matched. Their profile includes a brief description where they write about themselves and the skills they possess, and tools and programming languages they are familiar with (referred to as tags). You can also view their joining date, number of finished projects, and reviews and ratings left by previous clients.

Unlike other freelance marketplaces, Codeable doesn't offer variable prices on bids. You only receive one estimate, which is calculated by their system based on all offers from the freelancers interested in your project. In a shared workroom, you can then connect with and screen the skill sets of the interested experts in one place.

In the last step, after you have made the hire, you need to deposit the total budget of your project into a secure escrow system before the project begins. In the case of high-budget projects, your project can be divided into multiple milestones, giving you the flexibility to pay for each milestone as opposed to paying for the full project cost up front. Once you have made the hire and your project is private, you can communicate with your developer using the private messaging system available on the platform. To share your confidential information and credentials, you can use Credit Vault.

As previously mentioned, you only see one estimated price on the bids you receive. This estimate is based on a $70 to $120 hourly rate paid to the freelancer, after which Codeable adds a 17.5% service fee. Sample pricings are available on their Pricing page, to help provide an idea on how much you need to spend for your project. You can use filters like complexity (low, medium, high), urgency (low, medium, high), and project scope (basic, average, advanced) based on the complexity level, urgency and scope of your project. As you change the options, the guide price changes in real time in front of your eyes.

Payments are released from escrow only after a project is marked as complete. There are refund options available if you are not satisfied with the work you received. You can also take advantage of the site's twenty-eight-day warranty to fix any issues. If your developer doesn't deliver satisfactory work, then you will receive either a partial or full refund depending on the amount of work that has been done. The refundable amount is decided either between you and your developer or by the Codeable team through a dispute resolution process when you can't come to an agreement with your developer. Remember that the Codeable service fees are always non-refundable and only incomplete projects within a defined timeframe can be refunded. If you have marked the project complete, it indicates you are happy with the outcome of the project and your developer receives the funds. There's no refund beyond that point. To pay your developers, Codeable accepts all major credit cards, bank wires, and PayPal as payment methods.

Another feature of this site is Codeable team projects. Codeable Teams are full agencies working within Codeable, who specialise in larger and more complex projects. The Help Centre and FAQs pages will answer most of your queries. To discover more about the platform and get answers to further queries, you can also contact them via live chat support. Codeable promises to respond to you in less than seven minutes on chat during office hours. No mobile applications are available, so the website is the only way to use the platform. The platform is highly rated by developers and clients alike for its services as well as its design and user-friendly interface.

While some people like to browse through all available candidates, the fact that Codeable does this for you is good as it should save you time and effort, and is something that helps make sense of the 17.5% service fee you'll be charged on top of your budget. FreeUp offers a similar service.

Ratings:

- Facebook: 4.7 stars out of 5 based on the opinions of 119 people
- Trustpilot: 4.7 stars out of 5 based on 237 reviews

Highlights:

- Ninety-seven per cent of pre-vetted Codeable freelancers are WordPress experts with six-plus years of professional experience
- Internal matchmaking system to match with the best of the best
- Get only one estimate for your project
- Share confidential information using Credit Vault
- Secure escrow system and twenty-eight-day warranty to fix issues
- Live chat support: expect a reply within seven minutes during office hours

DesignCrowd

All things design-related: web, print, logo, graphics and more.

DesignCrowd, founded in 2007, is a global designer crowdsourcing platform with more than 900,000 designers, twenty-five to 100+ designs per project, over 300,000 completed projects and more than 1 million businesses. It is a community of designers mostly living in the USA, the UK, Europe, Australia and India, specialising in every design field. The most popular design services on DesignCrowd are logos, business cards, web, flyers, graphics, T-shirts, 3D, advertisements, applications, apparel, billboards, blogs, book covers, packaging, CVs, posters, menus, and brochures.

As this is a design crowdsourcing platform, the primary method to purchase services from the designers is by holding design contests similar to those on 99Designs and Freelancer. Design contests are run to get a number of creative designs from multiple designers, while One-Designer service projects are used to work with a specific designer. Design contests are best for medium-complexity jobs, allowing you unlimited designs from many providers. One-Designer jobs are suitable for low-complexity jobs with lower budgets usually ranging from $10 to $30, depending on design category or if you want to work with a specific designer.

First you need to select a contest package based on the number of designs you want, number of designers, revisions, etc. The basic package starts at $99, for which you get between one and three designs, and the highest contest package will cost you $729, where you get more than 150 designs. With each upgrade on contest packages, you get access to more features. You have the option to choose project upgrades while posting a contest. These upgrades will cost you additional money. Some of these include 'express turnaround' for a faster completion, 'private project' to make your contests private (so they can't be found on Google and can't be used as part of the designer's portfolio), 'top designers' to ensure three top-rated designers work on your project, 'featured project' for contest promotion, 'add website with domain and hosting' and more.

As well as choosing the budget that best fits your needs, you can allocate second and/or third-place prizes for the contest to increase motivation. You can also increase the budget for the first, second or third-placed designer. The minimum amount for a 'place payment', e.g. for second place, is $100. You can invite your preferred designers to participate in contests and the invites can be paid as well, meaning you can pay a certain amount to increase motivation. You also have the ability to choose a three, five or ten-day deadline. You can even host mini contests that are restricted to only five designers with positive feedback scores of 2.5 or higher.

For both contests and One-Designer jobs, you are required to deposit your budget upfront. At the end of posting a project, you select your favourite design and the winner is rewarded with the prize amount. In One-Designer jobs, the funds are released after you receive your design and approve the work. While a contest is running, you can interact with your designers via Manage Project by clicking on the Designer Discussion tab. During contests, you can broadcast a message that will be displayed on your project brief and your designers can respond to your message.

Guaranteed contests are those where you are obliged to pay after the completion of the contest. In the event you don't like any of the designs, DesignCrowd offers a money-back guarantee where you can request a refund within a defined period of time of posting your project. However, DesignCrowd will retain your posting fees of between $29 and $129, depending on your package, as well as any upgrade fees. In the case of guaranteed contests, you will not be eligible for a refund.

If all goes well and you decide to post another job, you have the option to start a One-Designer job with a preferred designer with whom you previously worked by buying their services directly from their profile. The budget of these jobs can also be increased if necessary. You can review designers' titles, their ranks on the platform, locations, positive feedback scores, total earnings, services packages, service categories and portfolios, all on their profiles.

DesignCrowd takes a standard 15% of all project budget, place, and participation payments from its customers, as a commission fee. Payment is via Visa, Mastercard, American Express, PayPal, or Stripe. Most of your queries will be answered by their Help/FAQ page, but if you have any further queries, you can contact the support team via email or phone call, plus there's a contact form available on their contact page. There are no mobile applications available for DesignCrowd, so the website version is the only option. The UI and design is standard but you might prefer the look of other design-specific platforms like 99designs or Fiverr.

For rebranding and white-labelling purposes, you need to open a business account and make sure you check the Agency Account option. Then, post your project and make sure your project is white-labelled by selecting the Make Project Private and Design Rebranding Functionality options.

Finally, there are a couple of sweeteners available on the site. Firstly, you can sign up as an affiliate and get paid for each customer you refer. Secondly, there's a free logo maker available on the platform which can be used to create a logo of your choice with unlimited revisions.

There's even an option as you are posting your job to have the freelancers sign an NDA direct from the website. There are numerous upgrades (effectively upsells) when posting your job, but I've never found them so distracting as to become a frustration.

Ratings:

- Trustpilot: 4.4 stars out of 5 based on 1,041 reviews
- Glassdoor: 4.6 stars out of 5 based on 14 reviews

Highlights:

- Design Crowdsourcing: Hold contests and receive unlimited designs to choose from
- Host mini contests restricted to top-level designers
- Business accounts for rebranding and white-labelling needs

- Free online logo maker
- Money-back guarantee if you don't like any of the designs

Envato Studio

Best for website development, apps, design and voiceover talent.

Founded in 2006, Envato Studio is a creative ecosystem of different websites providing creative digital services to millions of people around the world. It offers a freelance marketplace which consists of over 3,000 unique services to choose from with a community of over seven million designers, developers and creatives specialising in service verticals like logo design and branding, WordPress customisation, websites and programming, installation, ecommerce and CMS development, content and copywriting, online marketing, video and animation, and audio. On Envato Studio, clients are referred to as buyers and freelancers as service providers. Service prices range from as low as $5 to as high as $2,000.

There are three ways to purchase a service. The first option is to search for service providers using search filters according to your requirements, to find the best matching services. If you are looking for something unique or specific that you cannot find on your searches, a second option is to purchase a 'custom job'. For this, you need to send an enquiry message to your desired service provider using the Contact Me button on their profile. When you and the service provider agree on the scope and budget of your project, the service provider will send you a proposal for you to accept. The third way to buy a service is buying an express service, which is similar to the Fiverr gig set-up. These are quick installation jobs and do not include customisations. You can directly purchase express services from the Market download page, where you are matched with an expert within the promised timeframe. Each express service has predetermined scopes set by Envato Studio, and you should refer to the FAQs page to better understand what information you should provide for express services and what information you should withhold.

    While searching for services, you have unlimited access to view any number of service providers' profiles. Here you can see the numbers of jobs completed by them and the number of repeat clients. You will also find which service packages are on offer. Inside each service, you may find service extras which attract additional fees: a service demo, showcasing what the end product will be like and a brief service description. Each profile features a thumbs-up percentage, which represents the ratio of buyers who recommended the service provider by hitting the thumbs-up button against those who hit the thumbs-down button. Reviews left by previous buyers are also displayed, alongside ratings on turnaround, communication and quality of service. After your job is completed, you will have the option to review your service provider. The service provider will then be able to leave a response to your review.

To get started, click on the Order Service button on the service page of the service provider. Then, you will be directed to a page where you need to select the service extras that you need, provide a service brief, and enter your email and payment information. For payment protection, Envato Studio takes payment upfront from buyers, as do the majority of marketplaces. Your payment is held securely until successful completion of the job. After that, your payment is released and service providers can withdraw their funds. In case of disputes, there is a robust dispute resolution system in place that guarantees a fair outcome. This system ensures that service providers are paid fully or partially for their work if they deserve to be or provide the buyer with a full refund if they don't. Joining the network, purchasing services and paying your service provider attract no extra costs on Envato Studio. Payment is made via PayPal, Visa or Mastercard.

Envato Studio has an inbuilt messaging system and job management tools. The website is straightforward and user friendly. Envato's easy messaging system can be used to track progress and communicate during the project while providing timely feedback. You can find answers to almost all of your queries on the FAQs page. For further information, you can send your queries to the support staff. The Envato community is huge and is growing every day.

There's also an attractive referral scheme on Envato Studio that helps you invite your friends to buy services from the platform. For each new customer you refer, you will earn 30% commission on their first purchase.

Envato Market is Envato's digital marketplace. It's made up of a collection of offerings that include ThemeForest, CodeCanyon, VideoHive, AudioJungle and PhotoDune. In ThemeForest, you can find more than 48,000 WordPress themes and website templates, ecommerce templates, CMS templates, marketing templates, courses, blogging, UI templates, and much more. CodeCanyon is all about the code for your WordPress site: plugins, scripts, HTML5 and Javascript code and add-ons. It's all geared to save you from developing something from scratch and give you the functionality you need. VideoHive offers pre-made video clips that you can purchase for whatever use you have; AudioJungle is similar but for audio files that you can use as backing tracks or for specific sounds in whatever you are creating. PhotoDune offers a complete range of royalty-free photos from as little as $2 each or you can select subscription packages for unlimited downloads. Images can be used on your website and any other marketing material as needed.

Ratings:

- Trustpilot: 3.9 stars out of 5 based on 4,102 reviews
- Glassdoor: 3.7 stars out of 5 based on 80 reviews

Highlights:

- Huge creative ecosystem of Envato comprising Market, Placeit, Elements, Tuts+, Milkshake and more
- More than 3,000 unique services available such as logo design, branding, programming, installation, copywriting, video and animation.
- Services ranging from $5 to $2,000
- Robust dispute resolution system
- Informative FAQ page
- Job-management tools
- Express services for quick installation jobs and rapid matching with an expert
- Invite a friend and earn 30% commission on their first purchase on the site

Fiverr

A little bit of everything in pre-defined gigs.

I've used Fiverr many times over the last decade. It's now true that there are few gigs available for the original $5, but there is still plenty of good value to be found on this marketplace. As you can see gigs and reviews and examples of the finished products, it makes it an easy marketplace to work with and generally get the results you expect.

Most times I've use Fiverr it's been for things like:

- Simple logo designs

- Logo animations
- Christmas videos
- Voiceovers
- Image creation
- Simple video editing

Given many of the gigs show you exactly what they are going to provide, Fiverr is a marketplace where you can be comfortable in the timescale, quality and cost of what you're going to get. In my experience, there are very few surprises. Only 2% of my orders on that platform have fallen below my expectations.

Founded in 2010, Fiverr has a millions-strong user base and claims to have facilitated many millions of transactions. Instead of the usual system where clients post the job they require, instead, freelancers (referred to as sellers) sell their services (gigs) to clients (buyers). However, if you're unable to find what you're looking for, it is also possible to post a gig request of your own. While buyers can find help for almost any gig, the site is most known for graphic design, marketing and writing.

With gigs ranging from as little as $5 upwards to $995, services are categorised into three different packages, and in spite of the large numbers of gigs listed, searching through them is made easy with filters to prioritise delivery time, language, location and seller level. The seller level feature is Fiverr's tiered review system that rates freelancers based on their experience and work history, comprising Level One

Seller, Level Two Seller and Top Rated Seller. In addition to this system, a star-based ratings and reviews and system appears in a seller's profile.

Fiverr Pros are sellers that have years of professional experience working with top-tier clients on challenging projects. The crème de la crème of the Fiverr world, these applicants go through a rigorous vetting process where they are quizzed on their professional background, higher education, skills and notable past projects. Every pro gig is labelled with a pro badge, so buyers know immediately that they are dealing with the highest quality sellers available.

Another option, Fiverr for Business, allows you to create a team of buyers and share a common funding source. As the leader of the team, you can add a credit card as a funding source through your Fiverr account and then other members of the team can use the card to place orders.

Unlike Upwork and other platforms, there are no membership plans on Fiverr. Instead, a flat rate service fee of $2 applies to all purchases up to and including $40, then 5% on purchases above this price. Sellers can be paid via PayPal and credit cards, and just as you might have come to expect, an escrow payment system is available. Like the other platforms, in the event of a dispute between you and the seller, you can use their dispute resolution system, so long as you opted to pay via their escrow system.

The first of our Top Twenty sites to feature a mobile app alongside its desktop version, Fiverr has a good user experience overall. Fees are reasonable and all of the core features such as a review system, vetting of high-level professionals, escrow payments and dispute management are present. It even throws some extras into the mix, such as their logo maker tool which uses AI technology to create a logo that fits your brand, and their 'invite a friend' promotion that means after sign-up, both you and your friend get 20% off their next purchase up to $100.

When you encounter as many marketplaces as I have, you'll start to find many examples of Fiverr-type sites which have taken their core offering and rebranded it as their own. Some, like FiveSquid, are useful in their own right, and others are simply poor imitations.

Ratings:

- Trustpilot: 4.1 stars out of 5 based on 3,595 reviews
- Glassdoor: 4.3 stars out of 5 based on 181 reviews
- Play Store: 4.5 stars out of 5 based on 181,514 reviews
- App Store: 4.9 stars out of 5 based on 187,100 reviews

Highlights:

- No membership fees
- No need to post jobs – instead buy gigs from the best sellers
- Gigs starts from as low as $5

- Get access to high-quality pre-vetted sellers with Fiverr Pro
- Easy to search and filter gigs
- Offers great UX in both desktop and mobile systems
- Free online logo maker tool
- Affiliate programme offering you and an invitee 20% off his/her first purchase of up to $100

Fivesquid

Very similar to Fiverr, with gigs covering voiceovers, video editing and animation, graphic design, music and audio.

Fivesquid is a gig-based marketplace similar to Fiverr with a lot of good talent in place, and it is known for high-quality work at relatively low prices. I found it suited me better if I required UK-based talent, for instance if I needed a British voice for a voiceover.

Launched in 2011, Fivesquid is a UK-based freelance marketplace used by individuals and companies from over 100 countries. Here gigs are referred to as services. The marketplace caters to a number of service verticals with the major categories being graphic design, digital marketing, programming, video and animation, writing and translation, business and advertising, and more.

Clients are called buyers and freelancers are referred to as sellers. All sellers on Fivesquid can sell their services at £5, £10, £20 or £50. A service can be sold at only one of the four prices. Only the PRO sellers can offer services at any price, however, to keep things simple, one can only sell their services at prices that are multiples of five. These sellers have paid to upgrade their membership from free to PRO version.

To find the services of your choice, you can browse through different categories and subcategories. You have the ability to look at predefined services available at different prices and select the one you like best. On a seller's profile, you can view their last login time, overall rating (%), description, spoken languages, services, link to social handles, reviews, tags and more. If you open their services, inside each one you will find the service description, instructions to the buyer, expected delivery date, order extras that you can add with the service, and feedback from previous buyers on that service.

Browsing on Fivesquid is simple, however, you can feel the lack of search filters as you do not have the option to view the services with specific prices. The number of services you see on the browser is also not fixed and cannot be selected. The list goes on as you scroll down and there is no indication of an end point.

Signing up and purchasing services on Fivesquid is free. You can order a pre-defined service from a seller's profile, contact them for a custom order, or you can post a custom request by clicking on Post a Request inside the Buyer tab. While posting a custom request, you need to attach all the required information, which then will be available for sellers to see and respond with their quotes. You'll receive an email notification from Fivesquid when a seller sends a quote for your request. In addition to above, you can also purchase recurring services from sellers on a weekly/monthly subscription basis. Note that only PRO sellers can offer custom orders at any price and subscription services.

You will be able to browse through your applicants inside the My Requests tab. Once you accept a seller's quote, collaboration begins and you will be able to send and receive messages using the messaging system on Fivesquid by clicking on the Inbox tab.

You will need to pay in advance for the orders you place. The Service Guarantee feature works as an escrow system and ensures that you get the project completed. Equally, your payment will be refunded if it isn't. Payments can be made using PayPal or debit/credit cards. If you are a seller as well as a buyer and you have a balance on your Fivesquid account, you can purchase services using these funds. However, the Fivesquid balance cannot be used for subscription services.

Fivesquid charges its buyers administration fees for different ranges of purchase prices. For a purchase of £5 to £9.99, you are charged an 8% administration fee. The fees decrease as the purchase amount increases. The administration fees for price ranges of £10 to £19.99, £20 to £49.99, £50 to £99.99 and over £100 are 6.5%, 4.5%, 3% and 2.7% respectively. Purchases made using your Fivesquid balance won't be charged the above fees.

If you wish to cancel your order for any reason, you can do that by going to the My Orders tab then select your order and click on Cancel Order. If your seller accepts your request for a mutual cancellation, your payments will be refunded to your Fivesquid balance. However, orders that are marked completed are not eligible for refunds. If you need to cancel a completed **order**, you must contact their customer support team within fourteen days. If you wish to transfer the funds to your PayPal or bank account, you need to contact the customer support team for a full refund. If you use the refunded balance to purchase another service, you won't be charged any administration fees.

There are no mobile applications available currently. Conflict resolution is handled by the Fivesquid support team, who can be contacted by going to the Contact Us page and filling out the form. They say they will respond as soon as possible and within twenty-four hours.

Ratings:

- Trustpilot: 2.3 stars out of 5 based on 42 reviews

Highlights:

- High-quality services at very low prices, starting just at £5
- Use the platform as both Buyer and Seller with a single account

- No membership fees
- Service Guarantee ensures that you get a refund if your project isn't completed satisfactorily

FlexJobs

More like a traditional job board, but for remote and flexible roles covering a huge number of categories, from accounting to creative to fashion to HR, insurance, legal and telemarketing.

Just as its name suggests, FlexJobs, which was founded in 2007, focusses on flexible jobs and projects, and with more than 500 hiring companies and more than 25,000 jobs, it is one of the most popular online hiring platforms.

In order to stick to their ethos of flexible working, you are only able to recruit and hire for jobs that offer some level of flexibility, be it remote working, a freelance contract, part-time working or an alternative/flexible schedule. Any postings such as commission only or multi-level marketing jobs that require upfront payment from the employee are automatically filtered by the FlexJobs system.

Jobs can be posted in more than fifty different categories, including skill level, experience level and part-time or full-time. Location requirements can also be stipulated, for example, 'US nationals only', specific cities and states, as well as 'anywhere'. When a job post is filled, it is removed and the system updates to ensure freelancers see new job listings each day.

Referred to as 'employers', clients are screened to ensure they have a positive online reputation and good credentials. Screening also ensures that employers are genuinely interested in hiring and are not simply spamming. Once successful, employers are able to post five jobs for free. After this, they will need to subscribe to one of three membership package options in order to post more jobs: $299/month, $729/quarter or $2,699/year. With any of these packages, employers are able to post an unlimited number of job postings and search through as many CVs as they desire. However, you can save 19% and 25% respectively with quarterly and annual options. If a greater level of personalisation is required on factors such as employer branding, featuring the job posts at the top, recruitment methods and social promotion, you can use their upgrade options. With all the membership options, features such as dedicated account support, customised employer profiles, activity and data reporting, expert articles and resources on remote and flexible hiring, as well as savings on over twenty vetted employer services (such as WeWork, Dell, Zoom and G Suite) are thrown in.

When it comes to payment for memberships, Visa, American Express, Mastercard or Discover are accepted and a seven-day money back guarantee is offered.

FlexJobs is more of a job board than an online marketplace, so if you've looked at these types of systems previously in traditional recruitment, you'll feel right at home. The main difference from the other job boards is the focus on flexibility and remote working.

Ratings:

- Trustpilot: 3.9 stars out of 5 based on 26 reviews
- Glassdoor: 4.6 stars out of 5 based on 26 reviews

Highlights:

- Best for posting jobs that offer some levels of flexibility
- All membership options provide you with an ability to post unlimited jobs, view unlimited CVs, and dedicated account support
- Savings on over twenty vetted employer services such as WeWork, Dell, Zoom, and G-Suite
- Customised options for employer branding, social promotion and sponsored jobs

FreeUp

Web development, customer service, digital marketing and Amazon specialists are your core services here.

Started in 2015, FreeUp offers a wide variety of jobs, posted regularly, that includes admin support, marketing, writing, design, Amazon jobs, e-commerce, and mobile and web software development.

This marketplace has an extremely rigorous vetting process where just 1% of those that apply are accepted. This process starts with an initial application, consisting of short Q&As on the applicant's skills and experience, as well as often overlooked elements such as a typing test and internet speed/reliability. A dedicated team then decides who makes it through to the next stage, which involves a Skype interview where their skills and experience are discussed in a more detailed fashion. For those successful enough to make it to the final interview, applicants are introduced to FreeUp's best practices and communication policies via a fifteen-plus-page document. If they are able to demonstrate they understand and accept these policies, they are accepted into the FreeUp network. As can be seen, this is an extensive vetting process that few other marketplaces can equal or indeed even try to. It therefore offers clients a fair guarantee of a skilled workforce that is built up of both agencies as well as individual freelancers.

You'll find that the fees for freelancers on FreeUp are more expensive than the entry level for the likes of Upwork and Freelancer. The upside to this should become apparent in that the team on FreeUp look for the most suitable freelancer to meet your needs based on your job posting, fee structure, experience required and the location of your preferred freelancer. This makes it a little more like traditional recruitment where the recruitment company takes your needs, interrogates their database, finds suitable candidates, screens them and puts forward their best three choices.

FreeUp's users are spread all around the world with roughly 40% of the pre-vetted users in the US, a further 20% in the Philippines and the remaining in a number of countries. This may or may not pose a problem for your project, and it's worth keeping the user base in mind when deciding on whether to post a job here. If you're looking for a native British English writer, for example, it could be more difficult to find them on FreeUp. That's not to undermine the quality of the users, and depending on your requirements, this might not be an issue.

When advertising a job, you first provide details of your project and budget just as you would with any posting. You are then put in touch with a freelancer within one business day and are given the opportunity to interview them for fifteen to twenty minutes before making a decision on whether to hire or not. As one would expect, freelancers have different rates based on their experience and skill level. For an entry-level freelancer, pricing ranges between $5-$10/hour, rising to $10-$30 for a mid-level freelancer, and then upwards for expert-level freelancers to a maximum of $75 per hour. An estimated pricing table is available to view on the FreeUp website and when it comes to time to pay, FreeUp handles ACH, credit cards or PayPal.

While the design of the FreeUp website is functional and provides a good overall user experience, many of the other features that are a staple of other freelance outlets are not present. There are no dedicated messaging service, no mobile applications and no monitoring facilities that take random screenshots of your freelancer's screen. A 24/7 live chat feature is available to offer support to both freelancers and clients, and there are some genuinely useful features such as automatic linking with an alternate freelancer (should things not work out with the first choice), but with so many other important aspects missing, FreeUp comes up short on the feature front.

The previous owners were bought out by The HOTH in 2019, so with the extra backing and strength of a larger organisation behind it, I believe you'll see positive changes on FreeUp in 2021 and beyond.

Ratings:

- Trustpilot: 4.6 stars out of 5 based on 93 reviews
- Glassdoor: 4.8 stars out of 5 based on 117 reviews
- Facebook: 4.9 stars out of 5 based on the opinions of 61 people

Highlights:

- Choose from top 1% freelancers who pass through a rigorous vetting process
- Wide variety of freelancers: admin support, design, mobile and web development, Amazon, etc
- 24/7 live chat support

- Automatic linking with an alternate freelancer if necessary
- Estimated pricing table for different levels of freelancers

Freelancer

Best for designers, developers, writers, marketing specialists, VAs, legal and finance.

Freelancer reminds me of Upwork in its earlier days, as it's a marketplace where you get inundated with applications and it's a little overwhelming at times.

Founded in 2009, Freelancer is the largest marketplace by number of users and projects. Claiming to connect more than 45,000,000 freelancers and clients, quite simply, Freelancer dwarfs all other marketplaces.

Clients are given three options for posting jobs. Standard jobs are referred to as 'projects' and work much the same as any of the other marketplaces. 'Contests', on the other hand, are a little different. They require an extra fee but stand out in that they allow multiple freelancers to work on the same project at the same time. Once all work has been submitted, the client then chooses which they like most and makes payment. Finally, 'local jobs' allow you to post offline jobs for people nearby for services such as gardening, cleaning and babysitting. A number of upgrades are available for your job posts that incorporate many potentially useful features from urgent listings to private, sealed and NDAs, giving considerable flexibility all in one place.

As with all of the other platforms, ratings and reviews can be left for freelancers by clients and then displayed on their profiles. In addition to this standard feature, Freelancer gives extra ratings to its freelancers on criteria such as number of completed jobs, timekeeping and keeping to budget, as well as repeat hire rate and earnings score. Obviously, an ideal candidate would have high ratings in each of these areas, but this allows you to pay attention to individual elements as well if necessary.

Although Freelancer has a lot of things going for it, there are some aspects that can be a hindrance. For example, while the sheer number of users can be viewed as a positive aspect, it can also be a nuisance in that all of your jobs will receive an extremely high response rate. Many of these will be unsuitable, so you already have the job of sifting through a significant number of candidates to find those of interest. Fortunately, you're not obliged to respond to all of them.

The messaging feature is equipped with many options for communication such as text, voice, video and the ability to share files.

For hourly billed projects a time-tracking tool is available, but it must be enabled by your freelancers, so be sure to ask them to make sure it's switched on if you want to utilise it. As with other platforms, this will take random screenshots of your freelancer's screen that can be viewed by both parties. Beware that this is only available in the desktop version, so if your freelancer works in any other way, you will need them to track their time manually and accept the fact that there will be no random screenshots showing proof of their hours. It's also important to note that the desktop software isn't the most intuitive and as it offers a wide array of options and features, there's a learning curve involved that can be confusing for those new to the system.

An escrow payment system is available which is, as expected, the recommended method of payment. Provided that you use this service, named 'Freelancer Milestone Payment System', a dispute resolution service is available for the rare occasion that your project doesn't turn out the way you expected. There is no arbitration service available as with some other platforms, however, and the decision made by the dispute resolution team is final and irreversible. For other queries that don't require an official resolution, the Freelancer community is huge and offers user support 24/7.

Posting jobs and getting quotes from freelancers is free using this platform but you are charged 3% or $3 (whichever is greater) as a payment processing fee for each transaction for fixed-price projects. For hourly contracts, a project fee of 3% is applied per milestone payment. There is also the option to pay your freelancer with PayPal and debit/credit cards.

Ratings:

- Trustpilot: 4.4 stars out of 5 based on 5,876 reviews
- Glassdoor: 4.0 stars out of 5 based on 1,546 reviews

- Facebook: 3.4 stars out of 5 based on the opinions of 945 people
- Play Store: 3.4 stars out of 5 based on 47,196 reviews
- App Store: 4.5 stars out of 5 based on 1,100 reviews

Highlights:

- Largest pool of freelancers providing all types of services
- You can post local jobs to hire nearby freelancers
- You can hold contests and hire the best performing freelancer
- Large community and 24/7 support
- Lots of upgrade options available for your job posts
- Time tracking tool

Giggrabbers

Best for creative industries like design and writing, web development and SEO.

Giggrabbers is a freelance marketplace that opened its doors in 2015. There's a variety of specialities on offer from its growing number of freelancers, including graphic design, web design and development, social media marketing, search engine optimisation, content marketing and more.

Joining Giggrabbers as a client and posting jobs or projects (called deals) is free. Once a deal has been posted, freelancers can reply with their quote. After this, the client may then review the applicant's profile, which includes details such as their skills, hourly rate and previous work (including the total number of projects awarded to them and their gross revenue generated), along with a short bio and reviews from previous clients. In addition to this, Giggrabbers offers an alternative system, similar to online shopping, where a deal is created by a freelancer that can then be bought by the client or customer. Each deal contains information on the freelancer, along with what the customer can expect to receive, for example, 'You'll get a logo with three revisions,' or 'You'll get a copy makeover on one piece of content/website'. It's a different approach that may or may not suit your needs.

If you are short on funds for your project, you can even raise funds with Giggrabbers crowdfunding tools. You also get access to the Project Planner tool. With this, you are asked ten Yes/No questions before posting any project, which adds a task to your Project Planner wheel. You can select a maximum of eight tasks per project. After that you are directed to a page where you enter the project details, budget, number of hours per week (for hourly projects), location requirements, project duration, project title, category and start date. You have the option to sponsor your job post to reach out to more freelancers with $4.99.

Giggrabbers features a range of useful options, such as the ability to create a professional freelance team along with offering enterprise solutions to small businesses, larger corporations and non-profit organisations, as well as government bodies. Though the basic package allows posting of deals for free, in order to unlock the enterprise level features you will need a subscription.

Four enterprise membership plans are available, each upgrade including more features than the previous one. The plans are Bronze, Silver, Gold and Platinum, priced at $1,999, $2,499, $2,999 and $3,499 per month respectively. These plans include three, four, five and seven freelance specialists respectively. All four plans offer features like brand and marketing, social media marketing and search engine optimisation. Upgrading to the Silver plan from the Bronze plan will unlock content marketing and writing. The Gold plan includes all the features in the Silver plan plus photography. Videography and website design and development are also included in the Platinum plan.

Payment to freelancers can be made via debit/credit card and despite lacking escrow payments, a dispute system is in place for the times when things don't go to plan. The Giggrabbers team will review all information provided before making an irreversible decision, usually within five to seven days. For less critical concerns, Giggrabbers offers live chat and email-based support.

While the Giggrabbers desktop website is fairly user-friendly, there is considerable room for improvement, and I found some elements to be lacking. While a messaging system is present, it could benefit from careful revision to compete with some of the more complete packages offered by other freelance marketplaces. Giggrabbers also falls behind in other areas, notably the lack of mobile applications, time-tracking functionality, work diary and reports, and, most importantly, an escrow payment system. Community-based user support is also on the sparse side and though the community is growing, it isn't the best at the time of writing. For example, a search for web designers in the UK returned twelve freelancers and a search for writers in the UK returned just eight.

Ratings:

- Trustpilot: 3.8 stars out of 5 based on 7 reviews

Highlights:

- Free to sign up and post jobs
- Crowdfunding tools to raise funds
- Project Planner tool

Guru

Best for sales and marketing, programming, legal, admin, engineering, educating and training, design.

Founded in 1998, Guru is one of the pioneers of freelance marketplaces, and has grown to three million users and 800,000 clients. However, it is a contradictory site. Despite boasting 24/7 support on their website, their contact page suggests otherwise, stating that they are available Monday to Friday, 9AM to 6PM, EST. In addition to this, like rival site, Toptal, Guru is lacking mobile applications, which in this day and age is something of a necessity.

Guru implements what it calls a Feedback Score, which is their review system for rating freelancers. Freelancers are able to display the usual elements on their profiles, including reviews from previous clients, testimonials and a portfolio of their work in order to give clients an idea of their skills and experience.

For each job you create, a dedicated WorkRoom is created where you can manage the agreement, create and assign tasks, communicate messages, collaborate with team members and manage payments.

Once you have selected a freelancer, a Time Tracker is available to track and record billable hours. Random screenshots are taken of your freelancer's screen and are automatically added to the WorkRoom, allowing you to easily track your freelancer's progress.

Guru's escrow payment system is called SafePay, and if this isn't used, you will be unable to consult their arbitration service for payment disputes. If you find yourself in the situation where you need to make a dispute, once a decision is made, any amount in the SafePay program is returned easily. Escrow systems are obviously much safer for both parties, and Guru accepts credit/debit cards, PayPal and bank transfers.

Guru does not require a membership fee in order for employers to post a job. They make their money by charging a nominal payment processing fee of 2.9% per invoice. However, if you use an eCheck or bank transfer to make payment, you receive 100% of these processing fees back.

Overall, Guru is fairly basic in what it gives its users and does not offer the same features and quality as the likes of UpWork. It's not one of my favourite marketplaces.

Ratings:

- Trustpilot: 2.4 stars out of 5 based on 63 reviews
- Glassdoor: 3.8 stars out of 5 based on 40 reviews
- Facebook: 4.0 stars out of 5 based on the opinions of 70 people

Highlights:

- No membership fees
- Nominal service charge of 2.9%
- Get 100% service charge back if you pay using an eCheck or bank transfer
- Time Tracker and WorkRoom

PeoplePerHour

A fairly general offering including programming, writing, design, marking, social media and music/audio services.

PeoplePerHour is based in the UK and started in 2007. With almost three million freelancers and one million business clients, it is popular all around the world. The site uses AI-based search systems to match clients with the best freelancers for their needs. Beginning as a gig or offer-based marketplace, it now also allows clients to post jobs in addition to finding gig sellers. Most popular gigs on PeoplePerHour fall within the design, technology, writing and digital marketing categories. Gigs start from £10.

Freelancers are known as sellers, and they post offers or gigs. Clients can buy predefined offers from the sellers with offer add-ons according to their requirements. Sellers are rated using a five-star rating system. In addition, you can read the reviews from their previous clients and see their overall rating score, displayed as a percentage on their profile. You can also see how many times their profile has been viewed and how many sales they have made. Sellers are distinguished again according to their CERT ratings. The CERT rating ranges from CERT1, CERT2, to CERT5, with the topmost rank being TOPCERT, which includes less than 1% of the total freelancers in the network. You can also view the sellers' portfolios, social connections, endorsements and testimonials from colleagues and peers outside PeoplePerHour on their profile.

Posting jobs on PeoplePerHour is free, although they charge you 10% payment processing fees for each invoice paid. Technically, these are hidden fees because they aren't clearly stated in the main pages of the website and you might only discover them during your first payment. Many clients have complained that they didn't know about the fees. You can find the information on their Terms and Conditions page.

PeoplePerHour boasts 24/7 support for Anti-Fraud protection. They use identity identification by verifying their sellers' identification documents to protect their users from phishing, fraud and identity theft. After the work is done, you instantly own the copyright. An escrow payment system is in place to keep your initial deposit safe, and you release payments if and when you are satisfied with the work and have received all the agreed deliverables.

The communication between you and the seller takes place in a Workstream where you can exchange information, attachments, make payments, request a refund or raise a dispute. Disputes are rare but they may occur sometimes. For example, if you and your seller cannot decide whether the work is complete, you can contact PeoplePerHour support for assistance. If necessary, they will provide dispute resolution to determine whether the funds in the escrow should be returned to you as a refund because the agreed work was not delivered and/or whether the freelancer is entitled to partial or complete payment for his/her work.

There are mobile applications for using PeoplePerHour on both Android and iOS devices. The usability and user experience of the desktop site is good, while the applications are often rated low, citing how they are comparatively difficult to use. Unfortunately, time-tracking software is not available and you need to use other applications to track time or make some criteria in order to calculate the billable hours for the work done. This is obviously less important if you're buying pre-packaged offers like a 500-word blog or logo creation. For clients, there's an additional feature where you can send a discount voucher to your friends and you receive cash when they complete their first project.

Ratings:

- Trustpilot : 4.1 stars out of 5 based on 3,393 reviews
- Glassdoor: 3.7 stars out of 5 based on 69 reviews
- Play Store: 3.9 stars out of 5 based on 1,031 reviews
- App Store: 4.3 stars out of 5 based on 19 reviews

Highlights:

- Offers start from as low as £10
- No membership fees
- Buy predefined offers as well as post jobs
- 24/7 support for Anti-Fraud protection

Reedsy

Best for all things book-related, including editing, ghostwriting, proofreading and marketing, plus book creation.

Are you looking for a ghostwriter, editor, proofreader or all of the above? Reedsy is a great site to find publishing talent stretching from the above to book design, marketing and publicity.

Easy to use and with a talent base that's quick to respond, Reedsy lets you get your requirements posted with the minimum of fuss, then select the applicants that best suit your needs.

Receiving bids and working through conversations is a breeze and I've found it a positive system to use. I especially like how you can see the history of the talent you reach out to. You tend to find that people who use the freelancers on Reedsy leave a more detailed review than you find on many marketplaces.

As the freelancers post much of their previous work, typically as a link to an Amazon product page, you can look at published books they have written or edited and more. It's a great way, over and above their proposal and Reedsy reviews, to gauge if their style is to your taste.

Founded in 2014 and based in London, UK, Reedsy is home to over 500,000 authors and for more than 1,500 editors, 500 designers, 35 publicists, 40 marketers, 170 ghostwriters, and 30 web designers (all known as 'professionals'). These professionals represent more than thirty countries and have produced over 10,000 books.

Using Reedsy, you have the ability to hire the top 3% curated professionals to build a strong team and bring your book to life. There is no membership fee to use Reedsy, and you have the option to sign up as both author and professional. You can increase your exposure by creating and sharing your Reedsy profile, and as an author, you can evaluate the statistics of your profile views and followers. Your profile consists of your name, cover photo, short description, an overview, genres, languages, and links to Goodreads, blogs, portfolio and social handles. You can upload your books to your portfolio via Amazon or Google Play. You can download your subscribers/mailing list to a CSV file from the Statistics tab and use it for various purposes such as running email marketing campaigns.

On your dashboard, you will see different tabs like My Books, Marketplace, Requests, Statistics, Finances, FAQ and Settings at the left side of your screen. You can import an existing book or start writing a new one inside My Books with the help of a tool called Reedsy Book Editor. Inside Marketplace, you will find talented professionals for your editing, designing, marketing and ghostwriting needs. You can search the best professionals using appropriate filters and send requests to up to five professionals to quote for your project. On professionals' profiles, you will find a short description, an overview, their services and subservices, genres, languages they speak and write, certifications, work experience and portfolio with the aforementioned links to Amazon or Google pages along with reviews, ratings and response rate. Once you've found editors or ghostwriters you like, Reedsy allows you to invite up to five individuals to start a conversation and bid on your job post.

To start a contract, go to Requests and then to View Quote and accept the offer that you like the most by clicking on Accept Offer. Reedsy accepts all major credit cards and all payments are processed by Stripe. Reedsy charges 10% service fee for professionals and clients alike. As your collaboration with a professional builds, the service fees drop down. For transactions between $0 and $5,000, the rate is 10%. The rates drop to 9%, 8% and 7% respectively for transactions of $5,001 to $10,000, $10,001 to $15,000 and above $15,000.

Reedsy's Project Protection acts as an escrow system and if you're not happy with your professional's work, then you will be eligible for a full or a partial refund as deemed right by the Reedsy team. It is strongly advised that you keep your payments and communication within the Reedsy platform. In case of conflicts, they won't review payments or communication made outside the platform. They are only able to review conflicts that are reported within seven days of the event.

If you wish to cancel your project, you can do so without charge within the free cancellation period. This period depends on the project duration. For projects with a duration of less than one week, this is one week prior to project commencement. For projects ranging from one to six weeks, the cancellation period is two weeks prior to the project starting date, and for projects with a duration of six weeks or more, it is three weeks prior to project commencement. Outside this cancellation period, you will be charged a 20% fee to be paid to the professional.

No mobile applications are currently available. The design of the platform is desktop oriented and user friendly. There is a Reedsy messaging system to send and receive messages and share files with your professionals, which is fairly average. If you need help with anything, you can contact the Reedsy support team by just clicking on the Help button and they will respond quickly. Conflict/dispute resolution is performed by the Reedsy team and they will make a binding design which both parties must comply with.

Reedsy is packed with bonus tools, courses and features. One of these is the Invite a Friend feature, with which you can invite another author to the platform and you will both earn $25 of Reedsy credit to be spent on the platform. Inviting a new professional to the platform is more rewarding, as you will both receive $100 when the professional starts their first project on Reedsy.

Using the tools tab in the navigation menu, you will find a variety of tools including Title Name Generator, Character Name Generator, ePub to Mobi Converter, Pen Name Generator, Plot Generator, Short Story Ideas, Writing Contests and more. Other services that are available on the Reedsy platform are Reedsy Blog, Reedsy Learning and Reedsy Live. Reedsy Blog contains a wealth of articles on different topics to help authors learn about book publishing, marketing tips, etc. Reedsy Learning offers more than fifty online courses with new lessons delivered to your inbox each morning. Reedsy Live consists of a number of free publishing webinars.

You can submit and launch your book using Reedsy Discovery, and there's a Book Cover Art gallery featuring designs from Reedsy professionals. There's even a Bestseller Podcast series to listen to, and you can read Success Stories written by Reedsy authors. If you're feeling lucky, you have the chance to compete in Reedsy's short story competition called Reedsy Prompts with regular $50 prizes. I can't help but feel that all these extras produce more of a lifestyle than a mere marketplace, and it certainly helps to raise Reedsy to the top of the freelance publishing tree.

Ratings:

- Trustpilot: 3.3 stars out of 5, based on 14 reviews
- Glassdoor: 4.3 stars out of 5, based on 18 reviews

Highlights:

- Access to the top 3% of curated editors, designers, translators, marketers, ghostwriters and website designers
- Project protection: get a full or partial refund if you're unhappy with your freelancer's work
- No membership fees
- Quick customer support

- Free access to Reedsy's extensive collection of blogs, tools and courses
- Use the Statistics page to download your mailing list and run email marketing campaigns

ServiceScape

Best for editors, translators, graphic designers and writers.

Founded in 2000 with more than 293,000 completed projects and over 87,000 registered clients, ServiceScape specialises in the following services: editing, proofreading, translation, graphic design and writing. Editing and proofreading include services on academic papers, books, essays, novels, theses and stories, while writing include services such as blog writing, content, copywriting, résumé and CV writing, SEO writing, cover letters, and so on. Freelancers are referred to as professionals and employers as clients on ServiceScape.

    Before you can submit a project, you need to sign up as a client. To submit projects on ServiceScape, you then need to search and select a professional you want to hire, using the freelance directory . Then you simply click on the Hire Me button on their profile and set up your project. You have the option to purchase a predefined service package or create a custom project. If you set up custom projects, the professional will provide you with a service proposal that will have a unique price.

You can review the following items on professionals' profiles: average client ratings, client reviews, ratings graphs, amount of work completed on the platform, headshot profile photo, video introduction, languages, social links and service prices. Their availability status tells you if they are available.

It's easy to send messages and attach any files to your professional. To initiate a conversation and send messages, click on the Send Message button on the professional's profile. When you receive a message, you will be notified via email, then you can click on the message to open it and download any attachments. To reply, simply click on the Reply button.

Track Changes is a tool that helps you to see the modifications made to your document. Your project is promised to be kept confidential. After the work is completed, you can also ask your professionals for editing and translation certifications for an additional $5 and $20 respectively.

After you set up a project, you are able to modify, pause and cancel a project according to your project needs. You can also request your freelancer to do it for you. To cancel an incomplete project, you need to click on the Cancel button. If your professional hasn't yet started working on your project, it will be cancelled right away and you will receive a refund. If the project is still in progress, it is required that the professional also agrees to the cancellation request. To cancel a project that is complete, you should either contact the professional or contact ServiceScape and inform them about the reason for cancellation. They will resolve your issue and provide compensation to you or the professional, based on the situation and evidence.

Payment is via credit cards, US bank transfer, PayPal, Corporate Account, or an Invoice Account.

The Corporate Account differs from the client account as it is just a payment method. If you create a Corporate Account on ServiceScape, you will be the account manager by default. You will be able to see the interaction between your team members and the professionals on ServiceScape. Anyone else who will use your Corporate Account needs to register separately as a client, sign in using client account information and pay for projects using Corporate Account information. You have the flexibility to sit back and focus on other important things while your team hires freelancers. You can track all the activity with usage data.

You can receive a deposit bonus that ranges from 5% to 10% depending on the amount you deposit. The minimum deposit amount is $500. You can deposit funds using Visa, Mastercard, American Express, US bank transfer and PayPal. Invoices can be downloaded by clicking on the Invoice button. To refund a deposit, click on the Refund button. You can't process a refund if the deposit is older than ninety days or your balance is less than the bonus amount. You can learn more about the Corporate Account on the How it Works for Businesses page on their website.

ServiceScape boasts of their high ratings on eKomi, which they advertise on their website as well as on their social media handles. To get your questions answered and know more on how the platform works, you can contact them by clicking on the Contact Us button on their website and filling out a form. Mobile applications for ServiceScape are not available and you will find that the website version is simple but usable.

Ratings:

- eKomi: 4.9 stars out of 5 based on 4,624 reviews
- Glassdoor: 3.7 stars out of 5 based on 16 reviews

Highlights:

- Best for editing, proofreading, writing and translation services
- Get your team to hire freelancers from ServiceScape using Corporate Account
- Get 5% to 10% deposit bonus on the amount you deposit in your corporate account

Skyword

Best for storytelling: creative writing and editing, content creation.

Skyword is a content marketing platform that provides its software and services to businesses and entrepreneurs. It specialises in providing content marketing, social marketing and social analytics. You can find writers, videographers, photographers, designers and influencers for your content marketing needs. Skyword was founded in 2010 and with nineteen languages supported for content creation, twenty-seven countries supported for SEO optimisation, vetted creatives from fifty-nine countries and twenty-three different currencies supported to pay your creatives, it is one of the most popular content marketing platforms in the industry.

There are three software options available: Skyword360 for content marketing, Skyword Social for social marketing and Skyword Intelligence for social analytics.

Skyword360 helps you manage your content from ideation to finish with great optimisation tools. The software ensures on-time content production without last-minute surprises. You can hire writers, designers and creatives through their talent network, using filters for your search. You can search by location and specialty of freelancers. Freelancers' profiles include a brief description showcasing their areas of expertise and their niches, Reach score (out of 100), Resonance score (out of 100) and their portfolio. You can sort by region to find local experts, tags (keywords) and review portfolios to find the best fit for your business.

Every freelancer in Skyword is an expert who has passed a rigorous vetting process. You can create Request For Proposals (RFPs) to get bids from your preferred freelancers. Skyword promises that you will experience streamline communication and can track content assignments, automate payments, and even manage tax forms, using their content management platform, Skyword360. There you can manage your workflow by assigning roles for each member in your content marketing workflow. With CMS integrations, you will be able to publish your content directly to your website. You get the flexibility to build your content in the exact format you need, depending on what CMS you use, by customising templates for blogs, articles, videos and infographics. Integrations available for Skyword360 include WordPress, Drupal, AEM, Marketo, SEMRush, YouTube, Google Analytics, Shutterstock and more.

For content production and distribution, Skyword promises a three-layer editorial review process along with content creation guidelines. After you publish your content directly to your website, you can amplify the content, grow your brand and increase your audience using Skyword Social, which incorporates social media management, employee advocacy and social attribution software. Integrations and partners for Skyword Social are Marketo, Act-on, Facebook, Twitter, Instagram, LinkedIn, Feedly, HubSpot, Google Analytics, SalesForce, Bitly and more.

Meanwhile, Skyword Intelligence, their social analytics platform, provides the real-time insights you need to connect with your customers and get ahead of your competitors. You will be able to sustain content marketing excellence with unified performance analytics and competitive intelligence. Integrations available for this platform include Facebook, Instagram, Twitter, LinkedIn, YouTube, Tumblr, Facebook Ads,

Instagram Ads, Twitter Ads, LinkedIn Ads, Google Analytics and more.

Major services offered by Skyword are content strategy, editorial and creatives, data and insights, and training and support services. Skyword will conduct user training to get your entire team comfortable with the content creation process and other features while using the software. There are also numerous resources like reports, videos and toolkits available in the Resources page on their website.

Unlike many marketplaces, there are no fixed membership plans or prices listed on the website. Skyword offers you custom service and pricing according to your brand and the scale you need. You can contact them by clicking on the Request a Meeting button at the top of their website, where you will fill in a contact form to request a meeting. During the meeting you can ask questions to discover more about how the platform works, how to pay your freelancers, how to use the software and anything else that you need to know. Skyword offers their customers dedicated technical support for troubleshooting. The Skyword website has a good UI and is easy to use, with a visually appealing design. However, there are no mobile applications available as yet.

Ratings:

- Facebook: 4.3 stars out of 5 based on the opinions of 29 people
- Glassdoor: 3.1 stars out of 5 based on 104 reviews

- G2: 4.6 based on 110 reviews

Highlights:

- Content creation, marketing and social marketing with the help of talented writers, videographers, photographers, designers and influencers
- Nineteen languages supported for content creation
- Dedicated software available for content marketing, social marketing and social analytics
- A number of integrations available for each software
- Custom service and pricing based on your requirements

Toptal

Best for project managers, product managers, finance experts, designers and developers – more focused than many marketplaces.

Toptal is another unique freelance site that was founded in 2010, with a vision to let employers hire the top 3% freelance talent by matching them with the pre-screened Toptal talents in senior level jobs like product managers, project managers, developers, designers and finance experts. After you post a job, they will match you with the best fit, usually within twenty-four hours. It might take two to three weeks depending on the job skills required, but that's unusual.

As a first step, freelancers are required to complete a testing and screening process to ensure they're a good fit to join the Toptal network. Once this has been established, to ensure freelancers have a high proficiency of English and that their personalities are well-suited to working with western technical terms, Toptal conducts thorough interviews and insists on a testing and screening process to establish their level of expertise, experience, personality and professionalism. The freelancer's portfolio and previous work are also reviewed and tests are administered in their relevant domain to ensure their eligibility. In total, the whole process contains five steps and approximately 3% of applicants are ultimately accepted. It's quite clear then that only the best and most qualified freelancers use this platform.

Based on the skills selected, Toptal matches you with freelancers that have hourly rates ranging from $60 to more than $200. While this is certainly on the upper end of many budgets, the big attraction here is that of uncompromised quality. In addition to these hourly rates, there is also a mandatory $500 upfront payment due when you sign up that will be used as a credit towards your first invoice once you make a hire. There is also no escrow payment system, as your freelancer is paid on an hourly, part-time or full-time basis.

To combat the missing escrow payment system, you're given a trial period of up to two weeks to ensure you are completely satisfied with your freelancer. If after this period you aren't entirely satisfied, you won't be charged, and you can choose to part ways completely, or Toptal will find you another expert. If you choose to have a second chance, you then enter into a second week no-risk trial with the same protections in place. In total, you are allowed three trial periods.

As well as their website, Toptal offers mobile applications for both Android and iOS smartphone users. Like most other platforms, they accept credit cards, PayPal and bank transfers. They have a free time-tracking tool, TopTracker, which produces screenshots and also helps in invoice processing, with other features like activity level tracking and productivity reports.

Toptal offers email support or you can submit an online form via their website. While this is not as comprehensive as some other sites, the lengths Toptal goes to in order to ensure the quality of freelancers, combined with the protections they offer with up to three no-risk trial periods, it is certainly adequate.

Toptal is clearly positioned with a focus on quality and while the costs are potentially higher than other platforms, including a substantial upfront fee, many regard it as the best place to hire premium talent for a wide range of niches.

Ratings:

- Trustpilot: 4.6 stars out of 5 based on 1,161 reviews
- Glassdoor: 4.1 stars out of 5 based on 305 reviews

- Toptal Talent on Play Store: 3.6 stars out of 5 based on 40 reviews
- Toptal Talent on App Store: 3.8 stars out of 5 based on 10 reviews
- Toptal Client on App Store: 5 stars out of 5 based on 5 reviews

Highlights:

- Get access to the Top 3% vetted freelancers
- Best place to find top-notch developers, designers, product managers, project managers and finance experts
- Up to three no-risk trial periods
- TopTracker tool for activity level tracking, productivity reports and invoice processing

Upwork

Best for almost any service that can be provided remotely – one of the most comprehensive and developed marketplaces.

Upwork is the platform I use most often for my task, project and staffing needs. I have used it in its current incarnation and previously as Odesk (founded in 2003) and Elance (founded in 1999), before both joined forces in 2005 to form Upwork. I've watched it mature into a great platform for individuals and companies who want to outsource and freelancers who want to build their business and find new clients across the globe.

In its early days, Upwork was similar to Freelancer in that you would get inundated with applications for every job you posted. This was exciting at first, but soon became disheartening when you read the low quality of responses and realised that many were simply applications from people who would apply to any job at all, regardless of lack of skills or expertise. This must have put many potential clients off outsourcing, as their early experiences would have been poor, time consuming and frustrating. Happily, over the last decade Upwork have fine-tuned their marketplace, application and vetting processes, making the platform an excellent place to find the support you need.

Nowadays, freelancers have to pay to apply to jobs. While this is only a small amount, it does drastically reduce the number of spam responses you will receive. Upwork has also worked hard to ensure the rating system for freelancers is accurate and provides peace of mind. For example, in order to receive the higher ratings in the Job Success Score and the Top Rated or Top Rated Plus categories, freelancers need to build good reviews with a reasonable amount of revenue generated over those jobs. For example, freelancers can't become Top Rated Plus if all their jobs amount only to $10 or $40.

With more than twelve million active users and five million clients, Upwork is arguably the most popular freelance platform at present. While most users are located in North

America and South East Asia, Upwork boasts users from all over the world. The Upwork community is truly enormous, and it's highly likely you will find someone within this marketplace who can help with your project.

Signing up and posting jobs is free with a basic account, but for advanced and additional features, a membership upgrade to Plus, Business or Enterprise accounts is necessary. More than 8,000 skills and niches are covered by the many freelancers that work via Upwork in categories including software development, creative and design, finance and accounting consulting, operations and customer support. With a client account, it is possible to navigate your way through the recruitment process and build a capable and effective team.

The Basic plan, which is Upwork's free membership, allows three invitations to be sent but limits the overall feature set and doesn't allow several of the more useful features such as upgrading to a Featured Job, Talent Specialists or dedicated account management. If you're a medium-sized business that will spend $1,200 or more, the Plus membership is worth the asking price of $49.99/month, as it adds some useful features, such as access to Upwork Talent Specialists along with fifteen invitations to freelancers for every job post. For larger businesses or companies looking for a flexible talent programme that can complement an existing workforce, a further tier, Upwork Enterprise, is available. Used by companies such as Microsoft and Airbnb, it offers tailored solutions and dedicated support with customised pricing depending on the level of service required by the organisation.

Aside from the monthly membership fees listed above, processing fees of 3% per payment are applicable to those with Basic and Plus memberships. For those with Enterprise Memberships, this fee is higher at 10%. In addition, if you want your job to reach as many freelancers as possible, it can be sponsored, although again, this carries an additional fee. Payment can be made with Mastercard, Visa, American Express, Discover or PayPal.

Upwork features a number of systems that allow you to review potential freelancers before you even initiate conversation. A five-star review system based on six unique areas enables you to see feedback left by a freelancer's previous clients. The freelancer's profile displays their work history and a list of their skills and testimonials from clients outside Upwork, as well as their portfolio of work. Drilling down even further, housed in the profile is what Upwork calls the Job Success Score (JSS). Just as it sounds, this is a scoring system that measures customer satisfaction and can be used to give a good idea of the freelancer's ability. For freelancers that consistently perform well and maintain a JSS of 90% or more, a Top Rated badge shows off their reliability. Freelancers that work on larger projects and have longer term clients can earn the Top Rated Plus badge.

While having all these methods to review and recognise good work obviously benefits clients looking to hire, freelancers new to the platform can sometimes be overlooked and suffer due to a lack of reviews or a limited portfolio. For those in this position, Rising Talent badges provide a way of making themselves stand out until they have opportunity to develop a more comprehensive profile.

Once the freelancer has been chosen and a budget has been agreed, payments are made into an escrow system for fixed price jobs. So long as the freelancer meets their deadline and delivers all of the work as expected, payment can then be released. This gives an added layer of protection, to both parties, preventing problems from poor work, dishonesty or poor timekeeping. Alternatively, for hourly jobs freelancers can use a desktop application called Time Tracker to monitor time spent on a particular project. This useful tool creates periodic screenshots and notes to show what has been worked on, allowing the client to check the accuracy of the invoice. Also, provided the feature is enabled by the freelancer, the Work Diary allows the client to check up on the work being done throughout the project, which provides greater peace of mind. Along with these features and protections, Upwork also provides a space for messaging and voice/video calls, including their own technology and latterly Zoom options, which have been a good addition.

If problems arise between you and a freelancer or agency, the dispute resolution centre is the place for those rare situations where you cannot come to an agreement. There are different methods when raising a dispute, depending on whether the job is set up as an hourly project or as a fixed-price project. For fixed-price projects, you can opt for an escrow refund, whereas with hourly projects you have to file a dispute within a review period. A dispute specialist will then be assigned to resolve the matter. In the case that they are not able to make a decision, the American Arbitration Association becomes involved to settle the case. I've used this dispute facility once in the ten years I've used the platform and found it to be ineffective and not driven well by the person assigned to the dispute. I would say it was a disappointment and not what I would have expected of such a mature marketplace.

Upwork's full and comprehensive set of tools and features enables the freelancer to optimise their workflow while affording clients the ability to periodically check things are going well. In my opinion, this total package is by far the best of the freelance marketplaces for outsourcers looking for multiple types of talent.

Ratings:

- Trustpilot: 4.4 stars out of 5 based on 4,121 reviews
- Glassdoor: 3.8 stars out of 5 based on 305 reviews
- Upwork for Clients on Play Store: 3.5 stars out of 5 based on 1,405 reviews
- Upwork for Clients on App Store: 4.7 stars out of 5 based on 8,200 reviews

Highlights:

- Huge choice of talent
- Sophisticated review system
- Robust communication system
- Time Tracker for desktop
- Work Diary to view work reports and tracked hours
- Set up an agency and add freelancers, business managers and finance managers
- Manage freelancer relationships outside Upwork with Direct Contracts
- Great customer support
- Dispute resolution

Workana

Best for all the general services you'd expect including design, programming, writing, and sales and marketing.

Back in 2012, when it was first launched, Workana was known as a freelancing platform for finding freelancers from Latin America. The majority of freelancers are still from the Latin America but today, Workana is one of the most popular freelance marketplaces to find freelancers from all around the globe with more than 2.5 million freelancers and over 30,000 projects completed monthly. Top service verticals on Workana are IT and programming, design and multimedia, writing and translation, admin support, legal, finance and management, sales and marketing and more. You can use Workana in three languages: English, Spanish and Portuguese.

From entrepreneurs to early-stage start-ups, small and medium companies and large corporations, everyone can hire on Workana for their design, development, assistance and writing needs. The hiring process is straightforward. First, you describe your needs, specify the tasks, set a budget and deadline. Then, you review the proposals you receive and review the freelancers' profiles and portfolio projects. You can chat with them to further enquire about their skills and availability. Once you have selected a freelancer to hire, you need to deposit the total amount of the project's budget. Your funds will be held in escrow until the successful completion of the project.

Within freelancers' profiles, you can review short descriptions about them and what they offer, top skills, languages spoken, work history, certifications, portfolio projects, their overall profile ratings, ratings on communication, scheduling and quality, reviews left by previous clients, locations, number of completed and ongoing projects, rankings, gradings, joining date and more.

Based on their experience and quality of work on the platform, freelancers will be eligible for gradings after they pass the predefined requirements such as total income, recent income and number of satisfied clients, set by Workana. There are six grading classifications in total and these are denoted by a respective badge which is visible on the freelancer's profile. The gradings are Iron, Bronze, Silver, Gold, Platinum and Hero. There are also profile badges called Top 100 and Premium to demonstrate freelancers' ranking on Workana and their Premium membership plan.

Workana provides you with the option to sign up as an enterprise to add talent to your team, with the following features: 100% personalised support, hiring help, account executive, customised developments and integrations, customised contracts and billing, and commission decrease. You can use the Basic plan for free and as long as you like, with access to many features like unlimited freelancer search, free promoted projects and video calls. There are three paid plans available, which are Plus, Prime and Enterprise. The Plus plan costs $49/month and the Prime plan costs $99/month, while the Enterprise plan is a custom service with a custom price based on your business scale and needs.

To communicate with your freelancers and provide more information on the project, you can use the chat and video call functions available on the platform. You can also check the progress of the project. Once you receive the work, the freelancer gets paid and you rate the freelancer based on your experience.

For hourly projects, your freelancers can track the billable hours using the Workana Time Report application, which tracks their time and takes random screenshots of their work. You can view the tasks and hours reported on the project through the Workana Time Report on the Workana

Journal, which is a complete panel for report management and approval of hours.

To pay your freelancers, you can use credit or debit cards, PayPal, Mercado Pago, Payoneer and other methods depending on your country. With the escrow system in place, your money is refunded if the freelancer doesn't complete the work. In case of disputes, either of the two parties can initiate a mediation process. Workana then conducts an arbitration costing $10 and decides if you get the refund for the project or the freelancers get paid for their work. Workana's decision on an arbitration is final and binding, and cannot be appealed.

Workana charges you with 4.5% of the total amount you spend for both hourly and fixed-price projects as commission fees. Most of your questions will be answered by their How it Works and Help Center pages, or you can contact Workana support staff via email. A mobile application is available for Android devices but the ratings left by the users aren't overly positive. However, the web version of the platform is neat with a great design and a user-friendly interface.

Ratings:

- Glassdoor: 4.5 stars out of 5, based on 33 reviews
- Play Store: 2.7 stars out of 5, based on 3,534 reviews

Highlights:

- Fully-fledged multipurpose marketplace like Upwork, Freelancer, etc
- Supports three languages: English, Spanish and Portuguese
- Well-equipped communication system with chat and video call features
- Workana Journal for report management and Workana Time Report for time tracking
- Escrow system and refund for incomplete work

Zirtual

Specifically for virtual assistants based in the USA with college degrees.

Founded in 2011, Zirtual is a freelance platform that provides virtual assistant services to executives, entrepreneurs and small business owners. The platform has over 200 virtual assistants (referred to as 'Zirtual Assistants') from over thirty-nine US states, making it an all-American workforce. However, clients hail from around the globe. Business services, property services, real estate agents, financial advisors, property managers, start-ups, e-commerce, authors and agencies all hire virtual assistants from Zirtual to help them delegate day-to-day tasks while they focus on the more important stuff.

Maybe you need assistance in different types of tasks that you don't like to do, don't know how to do or don't have the time to do. You can choose Zirtual if you are looking for someone who lives in the US and has a college degree. Some of the most common services provided are email inbox management, calendar management, appointment scheduling, email marketing management, internet research, invoicing, expense tracking, data entry, transcription, event planning and website maintenance.

The Zirtual team accepts new applications as well as referrals from other Zirtual assistants who are already a part of the community. All applicants go through a rigorous vetting process. Following a basic interview, the Zirtual team asks them to make a short video of themselves or schedule a Skype interview to get a sense of the applicant's personality. After this phase, the applicant undergoes skill tests and provides sample tasks. The Zirtual team also performs a background check on the selected applicants and provides training in the top administrative tasks that clients require. Out of over 1,000 applicants each month, only 2% are selected to join the Zirtual team.

There are four different plans to select from on Zirtual. The first one is the Entrepreneur plan with a monthly fee of $449, for which you receive twelve hours of task work per month. Only one user is included in this package, and it is recommended for small tasks. For projects beyond inbox and scheduling, you can select the Startup plan, which costs $749 per month and provides twenty-four hours of work per month. Two users are included in this package. The other two upgrades are Small Business and Team plans, which cost $1,099/month and $1,499/month respectively. You get thirty hours of work and three users are included with the Small Business plan, and fifty hours of work and five users are included in the Team plan.

After you are matched with the best fit for your needs based on skills, time and personality, you will meet your new assistant during your delegation strategy call. If you feel that the assistant you are matched with is not right for you, you can request a different assistant. You will only ever be working with one dedicated Zirtual assistant. If there's something unique that they are not familiar with, they will get help from a fellow Zirtual assistant who specialises in that area. You can directly contact your dedicated assistant via phone, SMS and email to submit your requests.

The website is clean and looks professional, however, it doesn't provide all the information you need. There are no mobile applications available. The FAQs page is fairly brief and it's not enough to answer all your queries. Support or community pages are not available, unlike the bigger marketplaces like Upwork and Freelancer. For support and more information, you are invited to contact the Zirtual support group via email or a phone call.

This is clearly a highly specialised marketplace which can be a good thing depending on your needs. A potential drawback for UK and European customers is that they only operate during EST and PST time zones.

Ratings:

- Glassdoor: 3.4 stars out of 5 based on 157 reviews
- Facebook: 3.9 stars out of 5 based on the opinions of 7 people

Highlights:

- Best for busy executives, entrepreneurs, solopreneurs and business owners
- Find pre-vetted and trained virtual assistants with college degrees and relevant work experience.
- Work with one dedicated VA and if there's anything he/she is not familiar with, he/she will get help from a fellow Zirtual VA

99designs

All things design-related via high-quality freelancers.

99designs is all about design-related jobs and designers. Founded in 2008 and boasting more than nine million delivered designs from a community of more than 500,000 customers, it is one of the largest communities for its niche with many thousands of talented and professional designers.

While it is possible to post all kinds of design-related jobs, some of the most popular requests are logos and brand identity, product label design, website and UI design, as well as T-shirts and book cover design. To get these jobs done, 99designs offers two main options. Firstly, as with many other platforms, designers can search for the designer themselves and invite them to give a quote for the job. The other more common method is to hold a contest. As with some of the other platforms, contests involve a number of freelancers all working on the same project. Once all the work has been submitted, a winner is chosen by the client, who is then paid. At any given time, there are more than 1,500 of these contests open and from a client's perspective, they offer a great deal of variety and options for each job.

Four contest packages exist: bronze, silver, gold and platinum. Each package upgrade adds more features and, as you might expect, costs slightly more than the previous. There are also individual upgrades you can make to a contest, such as fast-tracking, blind and private contests and invite only, however these come with additional fees, so make sure they really add value before you proceed.

A simple but effective thing that 99designs does well is guide you through a series of specific questions depending on the contest you launch. For instance, if you're running a contest to design a book cover, you'll be asked questions including title of book, author's name, photo of author, genre of book, book blurb, and you'll also be asked to select cover examples that you like. I find this overall simplicity works well and means you get faster results than you would if running a competition on Freelancer.

During a contest, the initial qualifying round takes four days. At this point, the client picks some of the designers to move forward into the final round, which then takes a further three days. If after the qualifying round the contest isn't stopped by the client, the prize becomes guaranteed, even if the contest wasn't formatted this way to begin with. Payment is then automatically released to the winner or shared between the designers if the contest is left undecided.

For one-to-one projects, i.e. those where the client chooses a designer themselves without a contest, a platform fee of 5% per payment to a designer is charged. This, along with other payments, can be made via Visa, Mastercard, American Express, Discover, PayPal and SOFORT (region specific). With the secure 'pay-and-hold' system in one-to-one projects, you release the payment after the desired work is delivered.

With businesses in mind, there is one further option for working on 99designs: signing up as an agency. This Pro version costs $500 per year and gives access to premium contest upgrade features for free, along with an account manager who offers onboarding, insider tips and strategies, a personalised designer matching service and dedicated customer support.

Freelancers are grouped into three levels – entry level, mid-level and top level – based on their experience and notable past projects. As a client you can view their completed designs from past contests and one-to-one projects, as well as the likes and comments their projects have received. You can also view their reviews, ratings and the total number of contests they have won, number of projects completed and a responsiveness score.

While the overall design of the platform is attractive and user friendly, and some of the usual features, such as a messaging suite, are present, this marketplace is lacking a few other notable features. No time tracking and reporting system is available on 99designs, which isn't an issue as jobs are more project based. There are also no mobile applications available.

99designs offers reliable customer support with email and live chat support. Direct phone support is also available for nineteen countries.

Ratings:

- Trustpilot: 3.7 stars out of 5 based on 680 reviews
- Glassdoor: 3.5 stars out of 5 based on 51 reviews

Highlights:

- No membership fees
- Choose or create the best package and host design contests and select the best design
- Sign up as an agency and get access to an account manager, insider tips and strategies, premium contest upgrades and dedicated support
- Live chat support

- Phone support for nineteen countries
- Secure 'pay-and-hold' escrow system

Chapter 4: Steps to Success

You've discovered the many advantages of outsourcing and how it can make a real difference to you and your business. I've guided you on a selection of the best marketplaces available, how they work and where they may benefit you most. Now it's time to learn how to write the perfect job post to entice the talent, shortlist applicants, interview, shortlist again, and finally, hire your first freelancer. In this section I'll give you a step-by-step guide to getting started and transforming your business, while making the process as fast, painless and successful as possible.

The great news is you don't need to start from scratch with a blank sheet of paper. That method tends to result in people giving up and doing things the way they always have rather than benefit from the new way of doing things. If you're a complete newbie to online outsourcing, I'd suggest you work through each step in order.

If you've already been outsourcing and simply want better results, following the order is still recommended, although you can, of course, dip in and out of the sections that you feel you need most help with.

The steps to successfully hiring a freelancer are as follows:

- Preparing a Statement of Work (SOW)
- Writing a good job post
- Compiling interview questions

- Shortlisting candidates (pre and post interview)
- Onboarding
- Creating training guides for your team

While our steps to success go into considerable detail on the process to follow looking to build your team via freelancers rather than traditional recruitment, smaller tasks and one-off projects don't always require the same level of depth regarding documentation or the interview process. For smaller tasks you can cut out some of the steps and create a shorter SOW and job post than you would otherwise.

For instance, if your freelancer will only interact directly with you and their tasks are very specific, you might not need to think about training guides and onboarding.

Example tasks where you wouldn't generally need to follow the full process could include:

- Translating a page of text from English to Spanish
- Completing research on the top fifty law firms in the UK and providing the name and LinkedIn URL for each of the partners in those organisations
- Optimising a set of images for a website

You get the idea, I'm sure. Here the job posts should be able to describe in enough detail what is required of the freelancer, what the result should be and expected timescales, without creating a detailed SOW or conducting long interviews, onboarding and training. In these cases you want to select people with a fair number of reviews and strong ratings based on a number of jobs that don't all sit around the $10 mark.

Statement of Work

Preparing your first Statement of Work takes a bit of effort, but it's well worth it as you progress through your outsourcing journey. I wish I'd known this when I started ten years ago.

A Statement of Work, often used in its abbreviated form, SOW, is a document that details every aspect of your project. It is prepared after you have decided what you need help with, and before you start writing a job description to post in the freelance marketplace of your choice.

An SOW paves the way for the smooth running and completion of your project. It is mainly used in project management or in combination with a Request for Proposal (RFP), which is then provided to contractors or service providers with all the project information to ensure desired expectations are understood and met.

If you write an SOW for your project before announcing a vacancy for the job position, you will know exactly what you want, when you want it and how you want it done. Then, when you are ready to hire a freelancer, you can include the SOW for your job in the contract. After signing the SOW, the work starts and runs to completion as detailed in the document.

Paperwork is not a favourite pastime for most people, and is generally considered boring and time consuming. It's all too easy to skip it and just push on with the task at hand, i.e. finding a freelancer. However, without investing your time on this step, you will find deliverables do not meet your expectations or freelancers contact you frequently to discuss more details on what is next or how something should be done. If they have an SOW in place, your freelancer will use their time to finish tasks, progress milestones and work towards the completion of the project while you grow your business.

An SOW is unique to each project and its contract. However, one SOW can form the basis of another. Each one you complete makes it easier and less time consuming to complete new versions for future projects.

Each SOW needs to contain certain core elements. From these, your chosen freelancer will understand your expectations of the project and its parameters even before starting work. SOWs are typically written for projects that need to be submitted as a bulk single product or a series of deliverables/products with different milestones.

For example, a job for website development with a deliverable of a website requires a more detailed SOW than a job for a virtual assistant, where deliverables may not be as fixed and where the timetable and schedule are variable parameters. Before you start, you need to visualise everything about your project, e.g. when you need it done, how many milestones you want, what your expected results look like, and every detail that you think is necessary.

The more SOWs you complete, the easier you will find writing SOWs for your projects and the less time consuming they will be. Hopefully, they won't be boring, as you will begin to link this process with a successful outcome.

Below I have listed the steps every good SOW should include.

1. **Introduction:** In this section, you should include a brief introduction of your project, who will be involved, and what the end result will look like.
2. **Purpose of the Project – The Goal:** The goals of your project will be discussed in this section and it should cover why the project is getting done, what changes and benefits it will bring, and what it will add to your business.
3. **Project Scope:** The project scope covers the technical aspects of your project. It answers what needs to be done and what processes are required for the success.
4. **Tasks and Requirements:** Here you need to break the project scope down into smaller tasks and requirements. Tasks are activities that need to be completed to achieve goals, while requirements are criteria that make your freelancer eligible to perform the tasks. You can include hardware and software requirements as well if appropriate.

5. **Milestones and Deliverables:** Make sure you divide your project into different milestones and assign each milestone a deliverable that needs to be submitted within a fixed deadline. Don't confuse tasks with deliverables. Tasks are actions taken, while deliverables are the end result of tasks.
6. **Project Timeline and Schedule:** Here you need to create a timetable and schedule of different phases of your project, including the tasks, milestones, deliverables and deadlines for each milestone in this section. Mention the hourly work limit in case of hourly projects and also mention work days, holidays, etc.
7. **Reviews and Updates:** To make sure the milestones are completed in the designated time and deliverables are exactly as intended, monitoring and reviewing your freelancer's work is important. After each review, update the progress as you see fit and amend any future milestones and deadlines as required.
8. **Standards, Resources and Testing:** Define the standards for the hardware, software, tools and other resources to be used and the quality of the deliverables in this section. If testing is required, mention which tools will be required.
9. **Payment Structure:** For fixed-price projects, I urge you to pay after each milestone, while for hourly projects, you can pay at regular intervals of billable hours worked or on a weekly or monthly basis. Also

mention the payment gateway you will use for releasing payments if you're not using a marketplace with its own payment structure.

10. **Special Requirements/Miscellaneous:** Mention your special requirements if you have any, such as NDA, non-compete agreement (NCA), GDPR, intellectual property rights, hardware/software restrictions, exclusions, security issues or restrictions, post-job requirements, etc in this section.

11. **Communication:** Clearly state the communication tools you will use for 1:1 conversations with your freelancer, chat and team meetings, and what collaboration, task management, scheduling, and work tracking tools and systems are in place.

12. **Location:** If the location where your freelancer will work plays an important role, then don't forget to mention this. Define the region, time zone and home or office space requirements clearly.

13. **Definition for Success:** Make sure you define what a successful project is and how the end result/product should look. Try to explain in a visual way where possible.

14. **Criteria for acceptance of the deliverables:** Mention all the criteria and minimum requirements that need to be met for each deliverable to be accepted. Also include the criteria that makes a deliverable or the project unacceptable.

15. **Signature and Closure:** The signature at the end indicates the closure of the SOW and that the involved parties comply with everything written on it. Make sure the SOW is signed and stored in a safe place.

As you work through the above steps, ensure your SOW is detailed but easy to understand. Use simple language without jargon, and make sure it can't be misinterpreted. Afterwards, review and proofread it thoroughly to ensure everything is as it should be. Get a colleague to check everything over for extra peace of mind.

Writing an SOW is a complex process and unfortunately, you need to write a unique document for each project. However, you can use one SOW as the basis for another. There's no sugar-coating the fact that writing an SOW takes time. If you're pressed for that, why not take a look at my detailed guides at kevashcroft.com for some pre-made examples.

SOW Examples

Example 1: Content writer/sales copy writer

Introduction:
We are a dynamic team of web designers, graphics/video experts, marketing specialists and project managers who ensure our customers' projects are carefully managed and tailored to their specific needs. We are looking to expand

our services to include copywriting, which means we need a talented copywriter with a strong grasp of the English language to join our team. For the right person, this project can be a long-term opportunity for collaboration as a member of our team.

Purpose:
The objective of this project is to deliver great content and sales copy for our clients' copywriting projects.

Scope:
We will work on copywriting and content writing projects on a regular basis. As we receive new projects, we distribute and pass them to our team members. You [Service Provider] will receive the scope of the project and write great copy as required.

Milestones and Deliverables:
Milestones will be set before you start your work. With each milestone, you will need to submit some deliverables. The payment will also be scheduled according to the milestones and will be released after we receive the deliverables for each milestone as promised.

Tasks and Requirements:
Requirements are straightforward: you need to provide great sales copy/content as deliverables. You need to have impeccable UK and US English. You should be available to

work on various websites when required. You should be able to write website content that entices the visitors to the website with use of strong Calls-To-Action (CTAs).

Project Timeline and Schedule:
You will work with us on a few test projects. After that, if we see a good fit between us, we can extend our collaboration and welcome you as a long-term member of our team.

Review and Updates:
You are required to provide timely and regular updates on the progression of the project. We will be reviewing and evaluating your work regularly and will monitor the progress of your work on a daily basis.

Standards and Resources:
We will provide you with the necessary resources and tools to commence and complete the projects successfully. You are required to adhere to the necessary standards according to the project scope and provide great copy/content that is 100% original and plagiarism free.

Payment Structure:
Payment will be processed via [Freelance Marketplace]'s built-in payment system. You will be paid on an hourly basis as per [Freelance Marketplace]'s billing cycle. To track the billable hours, you will need to use a time tracker and take

screenshots/screen recordings while you are working. Generally, the freelance marketplace we use will provide the tool for this purpose. You will be paid $x to $x per hour based on various factors. Payment will be released after each milestone and only after we receive the promised deliverables associated with the milestone.

Special Requirements:
You will be required to sign an NDA.

Communication:
For communication, we need to use the [Freelance Marketplace] messaging system until the contract starts. After that, we can communicate via Skype and email. For task scheduling and management, we will use the Asana project management system.

Work Location:
Work will be performed at your home, office or whichever location suits you best.

Definition of a successful project
A successful project would be where the copy/content that you provide is 100% original, enticing and results in client satisfaction with little to no edits or rewrites.

Criteria for acceptance of deliverables:

Your work will only be accepted if it is plagiarism free. We use a plagiarism checker tool to ensure the content provided is 100% original. If the submitted copy fails to pass the plagiarism test, the deliverable won't be accepted and won't be paid for. The deliverables must be submitted inside the deadline. If you are unable to complete the deliverable inside the deadline, you should inform us beforehand and we will proceed based on the situation. If you fail to do so and miss the deadline, then your work won't be accepted and won't be paid for.

Closure and Authorisation:

This form hereby declares the compliance of both the client and the service provider with all the details mentioned in this document.

Authorisation		
Client	Signature	
	Name	
	Title	
	Date	
Service Provider	Signature	
	Name	
	Title	
	Date	

Example 2: Email list builder

Introduction:
I own a small business that provides website design services to clients in the UK. I am currently looking for someone who can build email lists for my business. The best fit for this job would be someone with past successful experience of email

list building, who can build a clean and validated email list by running email marketing and ad campaigns.

Purpose:
My goal is to have a large list of contacts who are interested in my services and with whom I can communicate via email marketing on a regular basis to provide value to them, build more business, generate orders and build new clients and referrals. These are people that need to sign up for our list – we can't simply add email addresses to our lists and spam them, as that is illegal. With this project, we wish to increase our visibility, sales and revenue. The end goal would be a verified and validated email list containing contacts that may need our services now or in the future.

Scope:
You [Service Provider] will need to set up email marketing campaigns using Mailchimp, Klaviyo or any software that you are an expert with. You need to be able to lead this project from start to finish. You might need to liaise with others and set up ad campaigns on Facebook, Instagram, LinkedIn and Google, and use software like Hootsuite for handling social media accounts. You should know the best way to build an email list for our business. We can create the landing pages if you aren't experienced with building landing pages, and we can create other marketing assets like images and video as required. However, you need to

create the strategy and email templates, use CRM software to hold the contacts and send personalised emails on a regular basis.

Milestones and Deliverables:
Milestones will be set before you start your work. With each milestone, you will need to submit some deliverables. Ideally, reaching a certain number of email addresses in the list would be our milestones, while an email list containing the target number of contacts for each milestone would be the deliverables.

Tasks and Requirements:
You need to build our email marketing lists as quickly and as authentically as possible. The list you build should be clean, verified and free from fake and duplicate email addresses. You must comply with GDPR. We have some lead magnets ready, but we don't know how good they are. We're open to your suggestions. Your job is to bring the ideas to us that you know are likely to work for us. We will constantly support you and provide you with any lead magnets and tools you require for the project.

The project scope can be broken down into following tasks:
- Research
- Setting up email and ad campaigns
- Holding contacts in a CRM
- Sending personalised emails

- *Review*
- *Report*
- *Make necessary changes and improvements and repeat*

Project Timeline and Schedule:
You will work with us for between one and three months. After that, if we see a good fit between us, we can extend our collaboration and welcome you as a long-term member of our team.

Review and Updates:
You are required to provide timely and regular updates of the progression of the project. We will be reviewing and evaluating your work regularly and monitor the progress of the work on a daily basis.

Standards and Resources:
We will provide you with the resources and tools necessary to commence and complete the projects successfully. You are required to adhere to using high-quality software and tools. The email list you come up with should be checked and validated using email validating software. If we find resources that would be helpful for the project, we will provide you with those resources.

Payment Structure:
Payment will be processed via [Freelance Marketplace]'s built-in payment system. You will be paid on an hourly basis as per [Freelance Marketplace]'s billing cycle. To track the billable hours, you will need to use a time tracker and take screenshots/screen recordings while you are working. Generally, the freelance marketplace we use will provide the tool for this purpose.

Special Requirements:
You will be required to sign an NDA and comply with GDPR.

Communication:
For communication, we need to use the [Freelance Marketplace] messaging system until the contract starts. After that, we can communicate via Skype and email. For task scheduling and management, we will use the Asana project management system.

Work Location:
Work will be performed at your home, office or whichever location suits you best.

Definition of a successful project
A successful project would be where the email list you build is 100% real and we see great results based on our agreed expectations with the ensuing email marketing campaign.

Criteria for acceptance of deliverables:
Your work will only be accepted if it is 100% real. We use an email validation tool to check if the provided email list is free of fake or duplicate email addresses. If the submitted list fails the test, the deliverable won't be accepted and won't be paid for. Email lists with fewer email addresses than we were promised won't be entertained.

The deliverables must be submitted inside the deadline. If you are unable to complete the deliverable inside the deadline, you should inform us beforehand and we will proceed based on the situation. If you fail to do so and miss the deadline, then your work won't be accepted and won't be paid for.

Closure and Authorisation:
This form hereby declares the compliance of both the client and the service provider with all the details mentioned in this document.

Authorisation		
Client	Signature	
	Name	
	Title	
	Date	
Service Provider	Signature	
	Name	
	Title	
	Date	

Writing a good job post

Writing an enticing job post plays an integral part in your search for the right candidate(s) for your job(s). Ideally, you should have your SOW ready before starting to write the job description. If you haven't already completed your SOW, I strongly recommend you do, as much of the information for your job post will come from that very document and makes this step significantly easier.

Think of a job post as an advertisement. People see it, think about it and take action accordingly. With the freelancing platforms we covered in the last chapter, people don't just search for jobs. Often, jobs drop directly into their feed and they apply only to the ones they are interested in. Make no mistake: the best freelancers get invited to hundreds of jobs. They are understandably selective and only respond to the job posts that seem interesting and are well explained.

Your job description plays a role in how your candidates will perceive you and your organisation. You are not just describing a job, but selling yourself and/or your business here. If you take the time to describe the job clearly, the freelancer will intuit that you are likely to know exactly what you want and will be easy to deal with. The quality of your job description gives the freelancer confidence in you as a client.

If you want to secure the services of a good, reliable and competent freelancer, writing short, boring or vague job descriptions is the last thing you want to do. Remember that while only the best written job posts attract the best freelancers, spending time now will save you time in the future as you deal with less unsuitable applications.

Once you are clear on what services you need and have a mental picture of what your ideal candidate looks like, then it's time to post the job vacancy on the freelance marketplaces. Follow the steps below to write an attention-grabbing job post.

1. **Log in to your desired freelancing marketplace:** This is your gateway to hiring the best freelancer for your job. Usually, it's easy to find the hiring section with the use of Call to Action (CTA) buttons that say 'Post your first job', 'Write job post', etc.
2. **Give your job a short but detailed title:** Job titles are relatively short in length (around sixty to seventy characters) but should have the power to entice the best freelancers to read the full job description. You need to make sure the title is full of keywords relevant to the job position.
3. **Divide the job post into subheadings:** Your job post should be easy to read and understand. Divide your job description into subheadings whenever it seems appropriate, e.g.:
   - Overview of the job
   - Essential skills
   - Desirable skills
   - About your company

Bullet points are often easier to read than paragraphs. The job requirements will have a direct impact on the level of detail you need to put into the job description, i.e. more detail is required for a new website project than a one-off social media image. If you have a very

long description to post, you can add the description in a PDF file and attach it to the job post.
4. **Be specific about required skills:** Mention all the skills and level of experience you expect from your ideal applicant. However, don't go overboard and try and mention everything under the sun. While looking for someone with multiple talents is not completely wrong, by doing so, you are potentially compromising the quality of work.
5. **List the software and tools the candidates need to have experience with:** Think of all the important tools/software that should be familiar to your ideal freelancer, distinguishing clearly between what's 'required' and what's 'desirable'.
6. **Describe unambiguously the roles and responsibilities:** To introduce clear expectations between you and the candidate from the start, you need to be specific when describing the roles and responsibilities for the job position. Your goals and intent should match with the freelancer's goals and their roles and responsibilities.
7. **Use the right tone of voice in your post:** The title and main copy should be written in a tone that fits with the culture, ethics and personality of your business.
8. **Build trust with the applicants:** It's essential to establish trust with the applicants even before you've spoken with them. For this, you should talk about your business, credibility, how you value your

employees and their career goals, and what makes you and your team good to work with.

9. **Add some screening questions:** In order to avoid canned or copy-pasted responses to your job post, be sure to add some screening questions at the bottom or in the middle of the job description. You can also ask them to start their application with a specific word or phrase to ensure that the applicant has read the post thoroughly.
10. **Identify the level of expertise:** Based on which freelance platform you are using, you might have options to select the level of expertise of the desired applicants when posting your job.
11. **Set required location and time zone:** If you need team members who operate in the same time zone as you, make this clear in your job posting. Also, make sure you state the hours you expect them to be available for your particular role.
12. **Payment structure and appropriate pay rate:** As previously discussed, there are two types of payment structure: fixed price and hourly. With the fixed-price structure, you pay the fees after the end of the project or after set milestones, while with an hourly contract, you pay at set points based on the number of hours worked by the freelancers. Decide what works best for you and this role, and specify it in your job description.

13. **Project timeline:** Mention the project timeline for the overall project in your job post. For hourly jobs, mention how many hours a week/month a freelancer needs to dedicate for the job position.
14. **Review your description and post:** After making sure all the requirements are included and are accurate, check for any grammatical mistakes or errors. Use tools like Grammarly or you can have it proofread by an expert. Once you are happy with your job post, you can proceed to post the job on the marketplace.

Job Description Examples

Here I have included four examples of different job descriptions, encompassing detailed posts for a Woocommerce developer and a content writer/sales copywriter, a shorter post for a logo designer, and a real-life post seeking a right-hand person for The JAR Group's own A.J. Lawrence, reproduced here with his kind permission.

Example 1: Woocommerce Developer

Job Title: Woocommerce developer/support
Category: Full Stack Development
Project Type: Ongoing Project, Hourly, Less than 30 hours/week
Estimated Project Duration: More than 6 months

Experience Level: Intermediate/Expert
Skills Required: Woocommerce, Website Development, Web Design, API, eCommerce Website, PHP, JavaScript, HTML, CSS, jQuery, Custom PHP, Git

We are looking for an experienced and reliable developer/troubleshooting/support team member for Woocommerce tasks and projects. If you only wish to work in one area, i.e. you are only interested in development projects, or you're only interested in providing support and troubleshooting experience, please let us know in your application, as we may be able to split the role between candidates who prefer to specialise in a specific area.

This is a part-time position. Some weeks there may be no tasks, some weeks there may be a few hours required, some weeks 5-10 hours and sometimes there will be projects which are 40 or 80 hours. We're letting you know this upfront so your expectations are in line with what we can offer.

Whilst we are not looking for a designer, IF YOU HAVE AN EYE FOR DESIGN – understanding the basics of what looks good and what doesn't with an ability to implement that – THAT IS A POSITIVE, so please make that clear in your application.

The scope of work will include troubleshooting problem issues and fixing them, adding or enhancing new features, constructing new or updating existing websites and online stores, connecting to other systems via APIs, setting up payment methods, delivery options and more.

Required skills:
- *Building new Woocommerce websites*
- *Working with existing Woocommerce websites*
- *Troubleshooting – identifying and resolving conflicts*
- *Editing and enhancing existing Woocommerce websites*
- *High-level HTML skills*
- *High-level CSS skills*
- *High-level PHP*
- *JavaScript*
- *jQuery*
- *API integration where required.*
- *Git*
- *Documenting any custom code you write or edit*
- *Ability to communicate effectively*
- *Understand written and spoken English to a high level to communicate with the team*

If you are interested in joining a small, growing team who take care of clients across the globe, please get in touch. Provide a strong cover letter which gives as much detail as possible on how you feel you can help, and what your experience is in relation to the above points. In order to be considered, please answer the following points fully by starting with their respective numbers below:

1. *Mention the word 'sausage' as the first word in your response. Failure to do this will result in your application being declined.*
2. *What is your general availability for work and what time of the day are you available? Base this on CET time, please.*
3. *Do you work weekends and if so, which hours? Base this on CET time, please.*
4. *Detail your experience in the areas we've listed. PLEASE NOTE: If you are interested in this job, don't tell us to refer to your profile or simply copy and paste generic information.*
5. *Describe any other experience you may have that could be of interest to us, as we have team members who develop and troubleshoot in multiple technologies.*
6. *Please rate your experience and ability on the items listed under required skills and do the same for any other skill you wish to tell us about.*
7. *Feel free to list anything else you believe would be beneficial to your application.*

Please take time to describe your experience and skills in detail for the above points. The better the application, the more likely it is you will make the shortlist.

We look forward to hearing from you.

Example 2: Content Writer/Sales Copywriter

Job Title: Professional writer needed for content writing and sales copywriting
Category: Copywriting
Project Type: Ongoing Project, Hourly, Less than 30 hours/week
Estimated Project Duration : 3 to 6 Months

Hourly Rate Range: $x to $x
Experience Level: Intermediate
Skills Required: Content Writing, Copywriting, SEO, Website Content, Article Writing, Blog Writing, Sales Writing, Sales Copywriting, Website Copywriting

Please do not contact us outside [Freelance platform's name].

About us:
We are a dynamic team of web designers, graphics/video experts, marketing specialists and project managers who ensure our customers' projects are carefully managed and

tailored to their specific needs. We are looking to expand our services to include copywriting, which means we need a talented copywriter with a strong grasp of the English language to join our team. For the right person, this project could present a long-term opportunity.

This project requires:
- *Copywriting expertise with good understanding of SEO*
- *Creativity and ability to conceptualise*
- *100% original (plagiarism-free) copy*
- *Impeccable UK and US English*
- *Ability to communicate effectively*
- *Availability to work on various websites and other resources when required*

You should be able to write website copy/content that entices visitors to the website to take actions with use of strong Calls-To-Action (CTAs). The projects would be regarded as successful when the copy/content you provide is 100% original, enticing, and results in client satisfaction.

The right person will first work with us on a few projects. After that, if we see a good fit between us, we can extend our collaboration for a longer term. You are required to have past, provable, experiences of successful copy/content writing. Please do not apply to this job if you do not have any prior experience and success.

If you are interested in joining a small, growing team, that takes care of clients across the globe, please get in touch. Provide a strong cover letter that gives as much detail as possible on your experience and how you feel you can help. In order to be considered, please answer the following points fully by starting with their respective numbers below:

1. *Mention the word 'sausage' as the first word in your response. Failure to do this will result in your application being declined.*
2. *Please share a brief summary of your experience and tell us about your most successful copywriting project to date. Ideally list three or four examples of similar work.*
3. *If you are interested in this job, please don't tell us to refer to your profile or simply copy and paste generic information.*
4. *Provide some examples of before and after where you've made a great difference to existing copy.*

We look forward to hearing from you.

Example 3: Short job description for a logo designer

We provide a range of marketing and web services to clients across the globe. We get many requests from clients asking us to complete logo designs as part of our service.

We have decided to offer this as a service and we're looking for a logo designer to join our small team. The logos we require are for business-to-business companies. We expect a logo pack at the end of each project, which will include web and print-ready versions. Pretty standard stuff!

We always provide a logo design questionnaire to get feedback on what's important to the client. This will allow you to be guided from the outset. We're happy to answer any further questions you may have.

This job will suit someone creative whose logos are original and concept driven, with a story behind why you've created what you have. We have an initial position available with a fixed rate of $x and we're looking to hire within the next 48 hours.

Points to note:
1. Please mention the word 'tomato' in your reply.
2. Please provide an example of your three favourite logos you've created, explaining why they are your favourites and what your brief was.

Have a great day!

Example 4: Real-life post seeking a right-hand person for The JAR Group's own A.J. Lawrence

The Opportunity:
Learn how to take over the world: Become a successful entrepreneur's right-hand person

Hi there, My name is A.J.. I've spent the last 20+ years as an entrepreneur in digital marketing, software and the cannabis space. Two of my companies have made the Inc. 500 of fastest-growing US-based companies. I've sold three of my past companies. Many of my old employees have gone on to run their own companies or take on executive roles. Four years ago, I sold my last company. Since then I've been an angel investor, consultant, coach and tinkerer. I live with my family in Southern Spain but travel frequently.

Now I'm rebuilding and scaling my various projects. The idea is to create real lasting value that makes an impact in other folks' lives. The organisation behind my efforts will be built as a remote operation from the beginning. I am looking for someone to be my right-hand person and help me refine what I have and grow these projects into one organised company.

This is more than being an intern or even a regular employee. You'll get hands-on mentoring and education, and as our work together grows, I'll also pay to make sure you are getting top of the line training from the best around. You'll be meeting and interacting with my network of other successful entrepreneurs from around the world.

I'm looking for someone who can grow into being a partner in my various businesses. You'll get profit sharing and, more importantly, equity as your capabilities grow. I'll also help you launch your business ideas if that is more your style.

The work would begin with a focus on marketing and then move to a full-on operations role. The day-to-day for the operations will be processes and systems intensive. Because the candidate will be the first hire at such an early stage in the company, there is the opportunity to design and shape these processes and have a large impact on the entire company.

The Role:
As a right-hand person, your missions will be very wide. Some of the missions you'll have to handle:
- *Project management*
- *Funnel building*
- *Content creation*
- *Marketing*
- *Client acquisition*
- *Reporting and client presentations*
- *and lots of other cool things!*

Grow to become a Chief Operating Officer
- *Have strong experience with funnels, growth and content marketing*

- *Hire and manage marketing team*
- *Work side by side with team to grow our user bases.*

Monthly salary will be around $3,000 to $4,000+ depending on experience.

You will need to be independent, have a true sense of responsibilities and be passionate.

If you think you're smart enough and you're someone we can trust, send us an email detailing your experiences and why you would love to join the adventure.

Looking forward to hearing from you!

Shortlisting candidates pre-interview

Once you've finished selling yourself to the freelancers, it's now the turn of the freelancers to sell themselves and their services to you. As the proposals and cover letters come in, it's time to shortlist the candidates who pass all your initial requirements and criteria for interview.

It already sounds quite daunting, right? I know exactly how it feels after posting your first job when, within a few hours, you are flooded with tens or even hundreds of proposals and you have no idea how to filter the best and most appropriate candidates. Don't worry! Like everything else, it's just a step in the overall process to work through.

Much like the traditional recruitment method, it's simply a case of narrowing down your list of applicants to some potential interviewees. The good news is that, depending on the marketplace you are recruiting from, it's easy to spot candidates that don't meet some of the basic elements of your criteria, e.g.

- Not enough hours worked
- Too few reviews
- Poor ratings
- Wrong time zone
- Outside your pay scale

As an example, the Upwork platform automatically lists best matches against your applicants, and partially hides those it feels won't suit. This feature makes it easy to discard applicants that don't fit your criteria by clicking the Archive option, which removes them from your main list and puts them into, well, an archive list.

You should plan to make progress as soon as possible, as freelancers are applying for jobs regularly and the best are also being invited to jobs on a daily basis. Wait too long and you may miss out on the perfect fit.

The points below incorporate everything you need to know while going through numerous proposals and making a shortlist to interview.

1. **Know how many candidates you want for the next round:** Based on various factors, your job post will get a few to around a hundred proposals. The first step is to know how many candidates you want for the interview round. Try to keep the number as small as possible, as interviews and second interviews take more time than you might imagine.
2. **Prepare a list of questions to ask them:** Ask yourself what you really want from the freelancers and prepare a list of questions. These questions can be related to the skill set required for the job, experience, previous projects similar to yours, personality, work ethics, available hours, and many more.
3. **Your job post itself is a great help:** Your job post is a great asset to discard numerous basic proposals that are not suitable for your job position. The candidates who really care about the job are more likely to write original cover letters focusing on the skills and experience that you want for the job post. Knowing that, you can easily discard the proposals if they:
    - Haven't responded with the phrase or word you specifically asked them to include in the proposal/cover letter.
    - Have copy-pasted their profile information into the cover letter.
    - Have sent a basic cover letter and not answered any of your questions.

- Have got a poor rating.
- Do not meet your preferred qualifications.

4. **Make a list of criteria that you will use to evaluate:** After the above step, you will have a filtered list of candidates but still many proposals to go through and decide on the shortlist. Based on the type of job post, you may have set your own criteria which you should follow at this stage. Some criteria that will help you to evaluate your candidates' experience and suitability for the role are listed below:

   - **Number of hours worked:** This is the total number of hours worked by a freelancer on a particular platform.
   - **Total money earned:** This is the amount of money the freelancer has earned using that freelance marketplace.
   - **Jobs in progress:** You can see how many jobs the freelancers are currently working on. This helps you understand the availability of the freelancers.
   - **Previous reviews, ratings and testimonials:** Almost all freelance marketplace have this feature available where you can look at freelancers' work history, reviews and ratings.
   - **Strengths and weaknesses:** These points highlight what they are good at and conversely where they lack skills or experience.

- **Additional skills:** These are skills that are not necessarily relevant to the job, but are something that is in your niche.
- **Working hours:** If you want someone to work in a specific time zone and during certain hours, then ask them about this if you haven't already done so in the job post.
- **Start time:** You need to make sure they will be available at the time when you are ready to start your project.
- **Completion date:** The completion date is crucial for a time-sensitive project. Make sure your freelancer will be able to complete your project within the specified deadline.
- **Hourly Rate:** A freelancer's hourly rate needs to work for both of you. If you're unsure about hourly rates, then look to work out a fixed rate for the entire project.

5. **Use some metrics to evaluate and compare:** As a metric for comparison, I suggest you assign a number value for each of the criteria discussed above or more. The range can be 0-5 or 0-10, or any scale you prefer. Calculate the average points for each candidate and arrange them in descending order.
6. **Don't lose sight of what you are looking for:** While going through the proposals, you should never forget your vision of your ideal candidate. They need not be the most popular or highly rated freelancer, but

someone with the desired level of expertise, skills, dedication and experience, and a communication style that suits you.

7. **Let Hiring Experts or Talent Specialists do it for you if you are overwhelmed:** The top freelance marketplaces feature an option where you can request assistance from a talent expert to shortlist the most eligible candidates. With their help in finding and shortlisting freelancers, you save your time and effort for other important tasks.

8. **If you have one, ask your assistant for help:** Provide them with questions to ask the candidates via the marketplace's messaging system. You can then ask them to perform a basic comparison in a spreadsheet using above criteria or more and highlight the best candidates for you to look at.

9. **Search and invite other eligible candidates:** To ensure you don't lose the best talents out there, many marketplaces have the option to find and invite freelancers to look at your job post. The Hiring Experts or Talent Specialists can also do this for you. Interested freelancers will send a proposal in response to the invite.

10. **Use available buttons to shortlist and hide proposals:** With most marketplaces, you can use buttons to hide or archive the proposals that you want to get rid of and shortlist the most eligible candidates. This way,

your dashboard will look cleaner and you have only the best proposals in front of you.
11. **Personality tests:** Personality tests can offer you a level of insight that may be difficult to get from a standard interview. There are various tests you can use which are offered in free and paid varieties like the DISC test or Myers-Briggs. While it wouldn't make sense to use these tests for someone who is going to complete a one-off task, they can be useful if you're bringing on a longer-term hire like a virtual assistant or marketing person.

Interview questions

A clear interview process helps you find the perfect fit for your job among the shortlisted candidates. The key to cracking an interview lies in the planning beforehand. From scheduling the meeting, introducing yourself and your company, and asking questions to closure, you should plan how you want the interview to start, progress and conclude. This process will guide you through what to include and avoid in your questions so you're ready and can make the most of the time available.

Writing interview questions can be tricky and time consuming. However, a little planning and execution will save you time and effort in the long run, and allow you to compare how your interviews have gone, making it easier to select the person you wish to work with.

The number of questions you ask and the depth you go to will be impacted by the job you are hiring for, so select the questions that make sense for your particular situation.

1. **Think as both interviewer and interviewee:** You should be able to guide the interview as per your plan and take control throughout its course. If you can put yourself in the position of the interviewee when you read your questions, it will help you perform a sanity check that the question a) makes sense, b) is a useful question to ask, and c) you're not repeating yourself.
2. **Use words that are easy to understand:** Your questions should be easily understood by your candidates and free from possible misinterpretations. Make use of simple words without jargon and only use acronyms that are common in your field.
3. **Set the correct tone of voice in your questions:** Your tone of voice in the interview will represent your company and the interviewee will evaluate you accordingly. Make sure you use the tone in your questions that best suits your organisation, and that clearly describes who you are and what you do.
4. **Set the mode of communication and length of the interview:** Give your candidates an indication of the length of the interview and what communication system you will use, e.g. Zoom, Skype, email, phone call, a marketplace internal messaging system, etc. Many marketplaces only allow you to use their own

communication systems until a hire is made, and indeed some may only allow you to use their communication system throughout the entire process, including post hire. It's important to familiarise yourself with the terms and conditions so you don't fall foul of the system and encounter unnecessary issues at this early stage. Ensure you are familiar with how your communications method works before your interview.

5. Ask them to set the date and time in their calendar for the interview so they don't forget when you will speak. If in different countries, clarify the time difference between you, and specify which time zone you will use.

6. **Start simple:** Start your interview with basic warm-up questions, getting to know the freelancer and their reasons for applying for the job. Once you feel your interviewee is comfortable, you can increase the difficulty level and depth of the questions.

7. **Ask questions based on their proposals and CVs:** You have already specified the qualifications and skills required for the role in your job description. Now, it's time to use your candidates' responses in the proposals and CVs to generate relevant questions to ask them in the interview.

8. **Their interests and hobbies:** To gauge how well they might fit your team, ask what their hobbies are and what keeps them motivated. Learn about their

interests and what they are passionate about. This all works towards establishing whether your personalities are compatible.

9. **Job-specific questions:** Ask them role-specific questions regarding their qualifications and experience. You can ask them to describe the process on how some previous role-specific tasks. Use screen-sharing options for real-time evaluation.

10. **Prepare follow-up and back-up questions:** You should have different sets of questions which can be alternated based on interviewees' answers to your preceding questions. Maintain a good flow and ask follow-up questions based on their answers.

11. **Address their strengths and additional skills:** Most likely, you have already asked the candidates about their strengths, weaknesses and additional skills in the job post or during the shortlisting process. If you haven't, now's the time to ask them. Also, ask how they can use those skills for you and how they will benefit your project.

12. **Try to get their honest answers:** Use vocabulary targeting honest and complete answers, such as 'how' and 'why'. You should ask for honest answers about their past experiences.

13. **Avoid questions that can be answered monosyllabically:** Your aim through the interview is to get as full answers as possible. Ask open-ended questions to get longer answers. You should avoid

168

closed-ended questions that can simply be answered using yes or no, which will not provide you much detail.

14. **Ask about their expectations, future plans and goals:** You want your business's need to align with your freelancer's future plans and objectives. That's the best way to move forward. Ask them questions to see if their goals and expectations match yours.
15. **If the freelancer falls silent, don't answer for them:** Your candidate should be able to come up with their own answers. Even if they remain silent for a long time, you shouldn't lead or prompt them to find the answer.
16. **Be a good listener:** A successful interviewer is a good listener. Listen to what the interviewee has to say and don't interrupt them while they are talking. Your candidates will feel more comfortable if they feel they are listened to with interest.
17. **Don't be biased and never ask leading questions:** Your questions should always be neutral and should not be inclined towards any opinion. Leading questions influence your candidate's opinion and make it more likely you will select the wrong person.
18. **Focus on your objective:** Never lose sight of what and who you are looking for. Remember that you are looking for the best match for your job, not the funniest one, the coolest one or the one most like you.

19. **Paraphrase your questions:** If your candidate doesn't understand your question the first time, you can paraphrase it and make it more understandable.
20. **Don't overwhelm your candidate with questions:** While questions are expected during an interview, the interviewee shouldn't feel bombarded. Let them finish their answers, listen carefully and ask transition questions or proceed to the next set of questions.
21. **Ask about their best work and biggest achievements:** Ask them about previous successes, biggest achievements and top projects, how they feel about those accomplishments and how they might tie in to your project in any way.
22. **Questions about their past jobs, clients, and experience:** How they performed in their previous jobs is a powerful indicator of their performance and potential success with you. You need to ask about their best and worst work experiences, relationship with past clients and colleagues, etc.
23. **Remain ethical and do not ask questions on sensitive topics:** Never cross the line and ask questions that touch on sensitive topics such as sexuality, gender, race or colour unless these topics are intrinsic to the job position.
24. **Don't go into unnecessary detail:** If you dig deep into unnecessary detail, you'll lose time and potentially alienate the interviewee.

25. **Questions to understand their personality and behavioural traits:** Ask questions that help you understand your candidates' communication methods, leadership styles, adaptability, motivation and willingness to learn where appropriate.
26. **Add light-hearted questions in between:** There's no doubt that you need to ask serious, difficult and challenging questions. But asking humorous and light-hearted questions in between makes the interview more conversational and fun. This also ensures that the atmosphere remains comfortable.
27. **You can find the same answer in different ways:** Ask the same or similar question in different ways and compare their answers to check if they match with each other.
28. **Questions with scenarios:** Questions with scenarios help you understand your applicants' methods, actions and reactions to different situations. Provide your candidate with a scenario and ask them what they would do and how they would react.
29. **Keep track of time to maintain a good flow:** Keeping track of a written list of questions may help you keep on top of the length of the interview. However, when doing this, you need to ensure there is a natural ebb and flow to the interview.
30. **Closing is also important:** Thank the candidates for their time and let them ask you any questions that

they have in their minds. Let them know if and when they will be notified about the selection or rejection.

31. **Use some metrics to evaluate their answers:** Immediately after finishing and while the interview is still fresh in your mind, use a five-star rating scale as a metric for evaluation and comparison of the candidates. You may even be able to adopt the star system during the interview itself for applicable questions whose answers can be rated as Excellent, Good, Satisfactory, Poor and Bad.

Shortlisting candidates post-interview

Depending on the role you're hiring for, it's likely you will move through the pre-interview and interview processes fairly quickly as you work towards building your much smaller shortlist. There is no specific rule as to how many you will take through to this final shortlist. You may take one; you may take three. You may take one, then complete your final interview and discover the chemistry isn't quite right, and you need to go back a stage to your other potential candidates. If so, that's okay. Your goal is to get the best fit for you and your job.

You'll most likely come out of the interview process with a gut feeling and a draw towards one or two of the candidates. It's important to take a moment and analyse the data you have.

How did they answer questions in a live situation, i.e. on your Zoom or Skype call? Were there longer pauses than you expected? Did their answers tie in with their initial written application?

You want to ensure you are as neutral as possible when revisiting the initial answers and comparing them with your interview with your candidates. Work hard not to select people simply because they like the things you like, or because you like their chat: base your views on the facts and data. Can they do the job you need in the way you need it done?

Communication is so important. I can't overemphasise the difference it makes working with people who communicate well. Your life, stress levels, hairline and quality and speed of output are all enhanced greatly when your team can communicate clearly and also understand how you communicate and what you need from them in the minimum of time. My point? Ensure you place a significant value on this one particular skill. If you've not managed to gauge their communications skills by this point, I urge you to take a step back and organise an audio or video call to do just that. This is especially important for longer-term roles and less important for a one-off job, like resizing a logo or providing a list of fifty Kent-based solicitors.

Use a combination of the scoring mechanism you've created, the quality of their actual audio or video interview if you've completed one, your gut feeling and anything else you can think of to make the best decision possible.

Finally, always remember that even if you don't hire them this time round, you may want to work with some of the people you've interviewed in the future. Be nice, and take the time to write a note to advise why they've not made it through to selection, however, you appreciate their time and efforts. Where there are people who have impressed you, ask them if they are happy that you keep a note of their details for any opportunities that may arise in the future.

Onboarding

Onboarding your freelancer is the process of hiring the freelancer with a proper contract in place and officially welcoming them into your team. Please do not ignore this step while hiring your freelancer; this is an important step to ensure smooth integration of the freelancer into your organisation whether you're a one-man band or a company with hundreds of employees.

You may be unsure what to expect and how the collaboration will work, however, it's often more difficult for a freelancer to adapt to the new environment than it is for you to bring someone new to your team, especially if you're prepared.

Poor onboarding can and will result in frustration and unsuccessful projects costing you both time and money.

With proper onboarding, you can focus on what you are best at. It also ensures freelancers start confidently and with high motivation, while reducing the time required to get them up to speed.

1. **Contract and agreement:** Most freelance marketplaces will have a feature for contracts. If not, have a legally binding contract in place. You should also have the SOW, NDA, non-compete agreement or any other important legal documents/paperwork signed by both parties involved before the work begins.
2. **Mutual expectations:** To ensure proper workflow and build trust, addressing mutual expectations is crucial. Practise open communication and don't hold back on asking anything you want to know, meanwhile encouraging them to do the same.
3. **Share onboarding videos, past achievements, websites, infographics and brochures to help your freelancer understand your company and your values:** This will ensure they understand your company, its culture and workflow, and can work as a team member right from the start.
4. **Schedule training programs and provide access to the tools and software they need to do their job:** If they require to use the company tools, give them access at the required user level. You may need to schedule training programmes and provide instructions to teach them the workflow in your organisation and how to use tools they are not familiar with.

5. **Sharing passwords and company information:** Be extra careful when sharing confidential company information and passwords. Also, remember that you should only share information that they need to know. Use tools like LastPass, Dashlane and Privnote to share passwords and sensitive information.
6. **Get their contact details and relevant information:** Depending on the type of job you've hired for, you may need different contact details for communication like WhatsApp, Skype, phone, email and social media messaging. If you require, ask them for certifications of academic qualification, training and job experience.
7. **Introduce them to your organisation:** You should arrange a virtual meeting for your team and the new freelancer. Introduce them to their respective department and the line manager (if there is one). Also let them know whom they should contact for help in case of issues and troubles.
8. **Communicate the goal with clear expectations for each deliverable along the way:** Make sure your instructions are crystal clear. Textual instructions can be confusing, so use audio/video calls to make sure your freelancer understands everything. Always stick with the plans defined in the SOW unless there are unexpected changes.
9. **Good communication is essential:** Communication is vital for the success of any project. Based on the project requirements, deliverables and tasks, you will

require different levels of communication. Ensure you are clear in what you are asking and they are clear on what they need to do.
10. **Monitoring:** It's important that you monitor your freelancer's work and job progression. You can do this with use of features of the freelance marketplace like Work Diary, Job Tracking and so on. Have daily check-ins and weekly meetings. Praise good performance and criticise poor work where necessary, giving examples of your expectations.
11. **Offer work benefits:** Work benefits are tried and tested methods of increasing the productivity of your freelancers. You can release a bonus payment if they perform exceptionally well and/or provide them with free tuition in their speciality, online courses, and so on.

Creating training guides for your team

During the onboarding process, individual requirements of your freelancer can vary widely, as can the amount of time you need to spend introducing them to your systems, way of work, quality procedures and any other processes they must follow.

You may want to remove yourself from this process as much as possible so that you don't have to sit (virtually) with every freelancer you hire and go over the way you work time and time again.

The best way to avoid this is to create training guides your freelancers can refer to during the onboarding process, so they can work through, learn and understand how they should do things in order to replicate your established processes.

Creating a training guide obviously takes time, however, you only have to do it once. This worthwhile step will save time in the future and gain a great deal more consistency in your business and results for your clients. I only wish I had done this at the start of my ten-year outsourcing journey, as it would have saved me time, money and many repeat conversations. It would also have given the early stages of my businesses more stability.

Good training guides ensure your freelancers feel at home and will be productive from day one. They will also view you in a higher regard and more professional light, which leads to longer term collaborations and better relationships between you.

Make sure you create training guides that show your freelancers how to do the tasks required, how to complete any reporting requirements and reduce the chance they will need to ask for clarification or need to do things twice.

You can create and share training material in various forms including videos, images, live lecture sessions, infographics and online courses. Select the formats you feel will work the best for you and your freelancers.

1. **Describe the purpose and objective of the training:** Every training guide serves its own purpose. Before you start the training, you should clearly describe its purpose, why it is provided and what the expected outcomes are. That way, your freelancer will get a better understanding of what they will learn in the process.
2. **Highlight the key points the training will take the trainee through:** Include a table of contents which covers the tools and software required for the training, what the evaluation metrics are and what the freelancer will learn and take away after completing each section.
3. **Link to other guides which will be useful for the trainee to learn from:** A training guide might not always be sufficient by itself. In cases where one training guide also requires some or whole portions of other training guides, you can link those videos, articles, news, infographics, etc, which will be useful for your freelancer.
4. **Example of a bad training guide:** A poor training guide is worse than no training at all. Overload of information, use of jargon and complex words, and repetition of the same things multiple times are some of the elements that constitute a bad training guide. Visit kevashcroft.com to find a complete example of a bad training guide.

5. **Example of a good training guide:** Companies that create and provide great training materials to their new freelancers while onboarding will see it pay off with their freelancer's enhanced skills, increased productivity and confidence. Ideally a good training guide is one which is interactive and has definite purpose, objectives and table of contents. It will also have clear and straightforward instructions that will answer most queries. To learn more about a good training guide, you can look at my detailed guides at kevashcroft.com for pre-made examples.
6. **What type of training should you create?:** Your chosen medium of training depends on what you feel is the best way to train your employees and what you feel is achievable. For the sake of time, perhaps you'd prefer to appear in a short video, or maybe the visual elements will be clearer in written format. Select the medium that suits you best, and then as you progress through your outsourcing journey, you can have someone else create them for you if you don't like to talk in front of a camera or if you're not suited to completing a voiceover when doing screen recordings.
7. **Tools to help you create your training material:** There are all types of tools available online that will help you create training guides. Based on the type of training you wish to create, you can select the tools that are easy to use, have good functionalities and fit with your budget. Screen capturing, recording and editing

tools such as Loom, Snagit and Jing can be used to record your screen while explaining what you are doing and send the video as a training to your freelancer.

8. **How to keep your training material confidential:** Tools like Folder Lock and AxCrypt will help you keep your materials safe in your system. You can also use Dropbox, Google Drive, and OneDrive to store your training materials in your cloud storage and share them in a confidential manner.
9. **Get feedback from your team:** Provide your trainees with survey forms after the completion of the training so as to measure the usefulness of the training and find any room for improvement. Creating and conducting surveys is easy with tools like SurveyMonkey and Google Forms.

Finally, don't try and get everything perfect before using training guides. It's better to get creating, start using them and fine-tune and create better ones as you go. You can find more tools to improve every aspect of your business listed at the end of this book in Appendix III: Tools of the Trade.

Chapter 5: Frustrations of outsourcing

Don't expect the route of outsourcing to be plain sailing. As with a traditional office-based team, you need to have strong systems and processes in place to give you the best chance of success. In fact, with an outsourced team, you need these to be even better, as you aren't interacting with your people face-to-face. You can't jump over to their desk and show them quite as easily as you can in a traditional environment, even though you can screen share and so on.

Don't think of this as a bad thing, though. It's actually one of the best things that can happen to you in building your business. The stronger your systems and processes, the smoother your business will run, the more consistent your results will be, and the happier you and your clients will be, as there should be fewer surprises.

Good communication with your outsourced team is crucial for your sanity and peace of mind; for getting your work completed first time, on time; for happy clients and also happy team members, as they will often need to interact with each other.

The simple fact here is that even with highly skilled people on your team, if your comms are poor, if your task descriptions are poor or if you provide poor briefs to your team, you'll get poor results. It's important not to blame the team in this instance and instead learn from your experience, so you can make the next job easier and better for everyone involved.

By the way, don't don't think for one minute that employing someone at a higher rate will ensure a better job. If your systems and comms are poor, you're likely to still get a poor result from a higher-paid freelancer with the added downside being that they will leave your employ far faster than someone on a lower rate who needs the work more.

Some issues in remote work are minor and can be solved quickly, while others decrease your productivity and cost you time and money. Some issues can be irritating or frustrating and can seriously affect the progress and productivity of you, your managers and your team.

In this chapter I discuss the most common frustrations you're likely to experience, why they may happen, and how best to prevent them or minimise their impact.

Trust issues

I can't stress enough the importance of trust in a remote business. I am not going to lie: trusting people that you don't know, can't meet and see regularly would scare anyone. But, with the right processes and systems, good job specifications, interviews, review checking, planned communication and efficient use of available tools and technologies, life becomes a lot easier. Slowly, you start to see the bigger picture and build trust with your freelancers.

Trust issues are common in business but they are generally heightened when you first start with a remote team. Despite this, if you can't build trust with your team, you will have a hard time delegating tasks, sending confidential documents and information or making any real progress.

With the advance in communication tools, screen sharing and collaborative working, it's easier than ever to work with a remote team and build the trust necessary while having the peace of mind that you can dip in and out of your tools to view progress and quality.

You should remember that your freelancers may be working from home and have disruptions due to various reasons. They might be disturbed by their kids or pets, or they need to do some housework or go out to fetch groceries. Don't jump to conclusions when you don't see them tracking time when they were supposed to. Work on the relationship to build trust and believe that they are doing their share of work, even if you don't monitor them all day. This is naturally difficult to do and likely goes against your instinct, however, my experience in this is over the last ten years has proven that the vast majority of people are trustworthy. The longer you work with your freelancers, the more trust you will build. If you don't build that type of relationship and you're always trying to second-guess what they will do or when you will get your work, you should terminate the relationship and find someone you can build that relationship with.

Measure the outcome quality and deadlines met rather than a traditional view of people at their desk from nine to five being the measure of success – unless, of course, you're paying them an hourly rate for a job where they need to be at their computer for a fixed time, i.e. customer service or live chat operator.

Just as no two people are the same, every freelancer who applies for your job won't be legitimate or trustworthy. Most of the time, you will know if a freelancer is trustworthy from the outset. When you ask questions, interview them or set test tasks during the hiring phase, you can evaluate their communication skills, body language, punctuality and responsiveness, and see if what they say matches their online profile or what they have written in their CV, cover letter and proposal. If you spot any conflicts, ask yourself if you feel they are trying to hide their flaws. Do you think they are lying about their skills and abilities just to get the job? With a proper interview process, you have a much greater chance of discovering if they will be a fit for the job.

There will always be a few freelancers who lie in their profiles, CVs and proposals to get the jobs that they don't have the skills to do. They might lie to the extent where they say they're an expert at something they even hardly understand. Most of these situations can be detected easily by asking them for relevant certifications, portfolio examples and past clients' testimonials, and comparing them and their answers to your interview questions and how you progress through your audio or video call with them. Ask them questions live in an audio or video call to also gauge the speed and clarity of their reaction and answer. Look for red flags where they contradict themselves, or where their example projects or existing jobs are very small. That way you can confirm whether they will be able to work on your project.

Even when you follow this process, invariably some people slip through the net who are unsuitable or incapable of completing your requirements. When you recruit new people and/or you're outsourcing a very important job, you should make your initial check-ins and milestones shorter to ensure things are going to plan and you can see the progress you expect. Even with years of experience in hiring and working with freelancers, I recall a few who have not been able to come close to delivering on the job, despite having confirmed multiple times the project was well within their experience and capabilities. Working on the basis of shorter check-ins for conversations and updates, I was able to see a number of issues that became apparent. For example, one freelancer was actually working a full-time job and looking to complete my project when he got home in the evening. His freelancing was a side-gig, which would have been fine, however, the faster check-ins also exposed the fact that he didn't actually know how to complete his assigned tasks. It transpired that this was a great example of dealing with someone who replies 'yes' he can do a job, but actually his 'yes' means that he is happy to take the job on. I cover this miscommunication in my 'Low-context and high-context culture' section later in this chapter.

Freelancers who avoid audio or video calls altogether should be moved through your recruitment process with caution. Gut feeling is always an important factor in any decision you make. Consider how good your gut feeling is and if it's been right more times than wrong – then go with it!

Poor quality work

With today's communication systems and time-tracking tools, you can connect with your freelancers and oversee their work and productivity levels almost as easily as you can in a traditional office environment.

Most problems are preventable and can be solved with proper onboarding, setting expectations and regular communication. Having said that, things can still go wrong due to changes in requirements or an overconfident freelancer who believes they are more skilled than they actually are.

Your project rarely fails when your employees perform poorly for just one day. You have the ability to evaluate their performance over time. If you see a gradual decline in their performance levels, then that's a matter of concern. You need to communicate with them honestly and openly as soon as possible. If you delay reaching out to your freelancers when they start performing poorly, it might result in project failure, which will cost you time, money, manpower and reputation.

Provide constructive feedback from the start. Reiterate your expectations, demonstrate clearly where their work doesn't meet your expectations and provide an example of what you are after, so there is no room for misunderstanding.

Depending on the root of the problem, you may need to provide training or access to some resources, courses or tools to help your freelancer. Of course, it may not be a problem that can be solved by training. Maybe their family circumstances have changed, or they're taking care of an ill relative, or there are other stresses affecting the quality of their work. It can help if you ask questions around these areas with as much sensitivity as possible. In my experience, good freelancers become great ones and also very loyal when you offer them help, flexibility and understanding.

If you continue to receive poor quality work from your freelancer, it's possible you have hired the wrong person for the job. It's better to identify this sooner rather than later. You might need to part ways and hire afresh.

While looking at the freelancer is the default option when things don't go to plan, it's crucial you also look inwards to yourself, your team and your systems and processes, in case they are the issue. If the management itself is poor, then changing freelancers will yield no positive results for you. You need to have a strong management that has systems and processes in place for every aspect of your business. Your projects should be planned properly where the potential risks, issues and complications are already calculated before the freelancer comes on board.

The best solution is always to make sure that you and your freelancers are on the same page from the interview phase to onboarding then to the project phase itself. Define their responsibilities, your expectations, regularly follow up, let them know the consequences of the project and how it affects your company. That helps give them a sense of accountability.

Long-term team members are the precious gems of your organisation. They are the all-stars that keep the company going and improving. They might see some rough phases during their stay. Try to connect with them personally so they know they can talk to you if and when any issues arise. The sooner you know, the easier it is to fix.

Feel free to delegate but under no circumstances abdicate. What do I mean by this?

The Cambridge English dictionary definition for the verb delegate is, 'To give a particular job, duty, right, etc. to someone else so that they do it for you.' In my experience, a lot of people either don't understand or aren't skilled in delegation. They view it simply as handing over a task with the minimum of effort and time spent, and hope or expect to get a good outcome.

The key here is making sure the person has all the information required, or the means to get the information required to complete your task. They also require any tools to do the job to the best of their ability, a reasonable timeframe to complete it in and a thorough explanation of your expectations and what you want the final result to be.

Abdicating, on the other hand, is simply handing over the job with the minimum of information and asking your team member to only come back to you when it's complete. People bad at delegating often confuse this with delegation and get frustrated when the task isn't completed as they expect. They blame the team member and often find themselves complaining at the end of each project that they can't find good staff.

It's tricky to hire mind readers in the marketplace, therefore, the greater effort you put into proper delegation, the more likely you are to retain your team, get great results and make more money. Delegate, don't abdicate!

Missed deadlines

Deadlines are an important part of any task or project for obvious reasons. Missing deadlines can cause time delays that impact other projects, reduce team morale and erode confidence in the team and your clients. They can even result in you having to pay a fee for a missed deadline or a project being cancelled, leaving you substantially out of pocket and with your credibility in tatters.

A deadline can be missed due to unforeseen circumstances and you can make allowances for that. Besides emergencies and unavoidable circumstances, there can be other factors where your freelancers may miss a deadline. These could include lack of communication among the team, poor delegation and distribution of tasks, conflicts inside the team, changes in the scope of the projects or an unrealistic deadline. You need to be honest with yourself about the reasons and make the necessary corrective action in your processes and procedures.

Yet, even with the best freelancer or agency in place and good communication channels, your freelancers may still miss deadlines. To minimise this, you must be proactive and communicate with your team regularly and check on their progress. Ideally, you'll have some form of comms or project management system in place that allows for the freelancer to update their progress as they go.

It's important to find out the major pain points before you take any action, and figure out what/who is the reason behind the missed deadlines. The following questions may help to pinpoint the source of the problem:

- Have you set clear expectations from the start?
- Is the deadline realistic and achievable with the available tools and resources?
- Does the problem lie with one consistently low-performing individual or is it the whole team?
- If it's the former, is the freelancer in question capable and adequately skilled?
- If it's the latter, do you have an adequately staffed team?
- Does your team understand the consequence of the project's success and failure?
- Is communication synchronised within your team?
- Is there any conflict within the team?
- Are you checking in daily or on a regular basis?

In team projects, it's rarely the case where only one individual holds you back and affects the progression of your project. Most times, this happens because of the whole team. If more than a few team members are missing deadlines, you need to make sure that the deadlines are realistic and achievable.

When a deadline is missed, you should reach out to your team, ask what happened and readjust parameters so that they don't miss another one. Part of that readjustment includes explaining the consequences of missing another deadline, i.e. they won't get paid, or they will be asked to leave the team. These examples are moving to the more extreme end of the conversations, however, they are required, depending on the situation. That way they will understand that missing deadlines is not acceptable. If you do nothing, they might feel that you are fine with missed deadlines and they will be prone to miss more in the future. You therefore need to reach out promptly, hold them accountable for their mistakes and take immediate action to make sure they don't miss another deadline.

Have systems in place to check progress. A great freelancer will notify you in advance if it's likely they will miss a deadline. You should make it clear that hitting deadlines is a basic expectation of their employment with you.

Missing deadlines regularly can be hugely detrimental to your business, particularly when a team is involved and others who regularly hit deadlines start to see if there are no repercussions for individuals who don't. While you may not like having awkward, difficult conversations with your freelancer or team, the sooner you do this, the better for you, them and your clients.

As I've already mentioned, look to understand any reasons for missed deadlines, be reasonable where you should, but don't hesitate to take action, whether that be withholding payment if you've had to find another freelancer to complete the work, or firing them from your team. You're not a charity; you're running a business.

Disappearing freelancers

For the freelancers, the best thing about freelancing is the amount of freedom they get. Albeit they are being monitored and time tracked if you have hourly contracts with them, but they don't have to deal with bosses/managers constantly coming up to their desk and asking about the project status. Freelancers get to manage and utilise their time in their own way. However, some freelancers can take your relationship for granted. They feel less obligated to complete the project on time. When you are miles away from your freelancers, some won't feel the same level of attachment to you as they would in a traditional office. And a lack of feeling of responsibility or accountability is never acceptable.

Misusing their freedom, freelancers can become unavailable, or take a long time to respond to your messages. Some disappear for days and respond infrequently. While infrequent communication in itself is a serious problem that needs to be solved, it can be more serious and potentially fatal for your project when your freelancer disappears without trace.

Freelancers leaving a project without any communication is rare, yet you can't eliminate the possibility that they might. The most useful preventive measure is to look at the feedback left by past clients for the freelancer's work. Make sure they do not have a history of leaving clients' projects incomplete.

When a freelancer leaves without any prior notice and does not respond to your email and messages, try to contact them using another communication platform. Look up their profiles on social media and see if they are active. Contact the customer service team of the marketplace you are using and see if they can make contact for you. You have a business to run and their unavailability will surely frustrate you, but do not jump to conclusions. They might be unavailable due to serious health or family issues.

If you do finally speak with them, ask their reason for the unavailability, and then decide if this is an acceptable excuse and if you are willing to try again. If you can't track them down or you're not happy with what you hear, then it's time to remove their access to confidential information and files, revoke their access from all of your systems, and remove them from your team. You have a responsibility to yourself, your clients and the rest of your team. It's important to be compassionate, but equally important to be a strong leader and make the difficult decisions when you have to.

As we examined in Chapter 3, most marketplaces have fundamental protections in place from hourly contracts to fixed-price options with escrow payment protection. You should contact the support team to explain what has happened. They should provide you with support and guidance on how to move forward with the contract.

Marketplace protection aside, to further prevent data theft and idea theft, have a non-disclosure agreement (NDA) and non-compete agreement (NCA) in place, and a legally binding contract as well.

Slow responses

The time taken by your freelancers to respond to messages plays a vital role in your business. Slow responses might halt your project for hours, days or more. It may even result in a project being cancelled by a client. This is where your communication guidelines will shine. Set strict communication expectations at the beginning to ensure important messages are addressed quickly without affecting the work.

Before you start working with your freelancers, ensure you have multiple contact points including email, Skype, phone, WhatsApp, etc, assuming their marketplaces allow communication offsite. (Some don't, with Reedsy being an example here.)

Ideally, you want a system in place to control your projects where the freelancer can make updates as he or she progresses. This is a far better method than asking for frequent email or Skype updates and will save you time in the future when looking for information previously shared.

Further expectations should be set around when you need your freelancer to be contactable. It's unreasonable to expect they will be around twenty-four hours per day, so be clear and agree on what works for you both. That said, some freelancers run virtual agencies and they may well have a team who will be contactable twenty-four hours per day, seven days per week.

You need to have effective availability and working hours for each freelancer. Set a time for an expected response within those hours. That could be five minutes, thirty minutes, one hour or even five hours. Initialisms like 'NNTR' and '1HTR' can be used in your messages, indicating 'No Need to Respond' and 'One Hour to Respond' respectively.

Building a culture of accountability within your team is essential. Encourage your team members to be honest about their availability. Tell them how they should respond if they are out, busy doing other work or are working on the answers to the questions they were asked.

It's important to understand why a freelancer is being slow to respond. If their reasoning makes sense, i.e. they are working on another task for you and you didn't explain you required an urgent response, or if you've not laid out any expectations at the outset, you can hardly give them a hard time for not responding when you 'think' they should.

If, however, they are slow to respond and you've covered all your expectations at the outset and had agreement from them that they are happy to work within those expectations, you need to make it clear, as soon as possible, exactly what you expect and reiterate that they have agreed in advance to work within the timescales you've set out.

It's fine to give second chances, especially if you are bedding-in a new team member, but if you find they are simply not following your agreed timescales – and you have made it clear you expect their adherence to the agreement during your work together – you should start to look for someone who can.

If this situation occurs with someone in your team who is normally great at responding when you've agreed, you should take time to consider what may have changed, whether that be in the job, your relationship with the freelancer or the freelancer's relationship with others in your business. Also look to what may have changed in their personal life that could be affecting this once smooth part of your relationship.

Perhaps they now have more commitments or responsibilities, and you may be able to be flexible with them on response times so as to retain them as a valued member of your team. In reality, this is no different to how you might make exceptions for a traditional offline team.

Half-finished projects

A half-finished project easily rates as one of the most frustrating and costly experiences for any client. An incomplete project is often worse than no project, given the time you'll have invested in preparing the SOW, listing the job description, interviewing, hiring, onboarding, making initial payments and so on.

There are many reasons why you can end up with a half-finished project. On your side this might be because you run out of budget, for example. On your freelancer's side it might be because they can't complete the job technically, they are running multiple projects simultaneously, they get ill or they get a better job offer somewhere else and leave midway through. Sometimes, your project might remain unfinished due to unrealistic deadlines.

To avoid this, setting clear milestones, deadlines and making sure you are on the same page about the requirements and expectations is the best solution. Make it clear in the agreement that you won't be paying for a half-finished project. Ask your freelancer to complete the project in order to be eligible for full payment. If you suspect they won't be able to complete your project, you should cut your losses and move on, by hiring a new freelancer who is more likely to finish your project within the deadline.

Ensure your freelancer's progress is clearly documented throughout, and set up in such a way that another freelancer would be able to take over at short notice if necessary. Ask them to detail how they will do this right at the beginning, in their job application or interview.

In the early stages of your freelancing experience, you may ask them to document and detail all their work in their own way, but over time you should create your own system for this and have your freelancer work within your system and guidelines, so you and your team are consistent and standardised.

The better you become at creating a good SOW, building your training guides, dealing with slow responses, missed deadlines and poor comms, the less likely you are to find yourself in this situation. The sooner you have freelancers document their work in your standardised systems, the less impact this situation will have on your business, as other members of your team or new team members you bring on board can familiarise themselves with your systems, check out the work completed so far and then move forward with the project for you.

Team conflicts

In a traditional office where employees regularly meet, work at nearby desks and interact a number of times daily, employee conflict can be a problem. Lack of visibility and physical attachment in a remote team will naturally see far fewer conflicts, but you cannot overlook the possibilities in this department.

Some business owners believe that conflict is important and even necessary for any company. The CEO of Zapier, Wade Foster, suggests that a business needs conflicts in opinions, beliefs and techniques to foster diversity in opinions. I don't believe you need conflict as it's defined in the dictionary, but I do believe a welcome and open exchange of views from the team will certainly enhance the projects you work on and will generate ideas and inspiration that you may otherwise miss. While small conflicts are to be expected and are usually easily solvable, you need to be proactive to resolve deeper conflicts that may threaten to halt the project's progression or damage the team you have built.

The most common cause of conflict in a remote team is miscommunication. Make sure to set clear communication guidelines and protocols that your freelancers follow strictly. Other issues that can result in a team conflict include poor work division and distribution, favouritism, geographical and language barriers, absence of hierarchy of management and reporting, unclear expectations and responsibilities, and lack of transparency and visibility.

To best avoid conflict, try to keep everyone on the same page. Manage responsibilities and expectations clearly. Encourage team-building activities, sessions and meetings. Discuss movies, music, news and sports in a separate thread in your communication platform to build and boost team bonding and morale. In case of unresolvable conflicts, encourage your freelancers to come to you rather than engaging in an unnecessary conflict with their colleague.

You should have a conflict resolution plan in place. Before you proceed to resolve any conflict, try to find the root cause and identify the members involved. Do not involve your entire team in the conflict resolution process.

Have a 1:1 conversation with the people involved. Listen to everyone's story, gather relevant details, compare versions of events and then gather everyone at one place with a video call where you can go over all the information together and you can see and interpret body language and emotions.

The best result you can hope for is that when you talk through the situation and entertain feedback, both parties see there is more common ground between them than there is disagreement, and they operate in a reasonable and clear-headed manner. If that doesn't happen, you effectively need to act as the arbiter and make a decision on what you feel is the best way to progress for all. You need to remember to be open minded, fair and give everyone a chance, but ultimately it's your business, and the people you pay need to work in the best way possible to suit you.

Conflict management should be focused on achieving common goals, resulting in a fair situation for all the parties involved if at all possible.

Last but not the least, do not forget to address the diversity in culture, language and location in your team. There can be occasions where conflicts might arise due to these differences. Nobody in your team should abuse, humiliate, embarrass or do something to create discomfort among other team members. To prevent this, have strict policies enforced with consequences for the breach of the rules, which include the ultimate consequence of being fired. To compensate for communication problems due to lingual barriers, practise written forms of communication and make sure to document everything as much as possible.

Having run traditional businesses for over twenty years and virtual business for the last ten, I can say hand on heart that the number of conflicts and small but time-consuming issues are infinitesimal in a virtual business compared with a traditional one.

Monitoring performance

Performance is the key to success. You need to ensure your freelancers are productive and perform well at what they do for your project's success. If you fail to monitor their performance, evaluate and review their work, they will most likely take you less seriously and think they can do as they please.

While micromanaging is never a good idea, this doesn't mean you shouldn't care about your freelancers' work and time they track. If you're concerned about their performance, put your freelancers on watch mode. You need to keep a close eye on their time logged, their quality of work, their responsiveness and so on with a view to making a quick decision on what to do and how to deal with the issues.

If you feel your freelancer's performance isn't meeting expectations, hire another freelancer to complete some similar tasks and compare their results. It may be time to say goodbye to your original hire.

Miscommunication

A huge frustration often appears in the form of having to explain the same things over and over again. This can range from where to find things and how to do things, to what type of information to include in feedback and what to check before sending work back.

The ideal way to stop this frustration, which eats away at your patience and profit margin, is to ensure you have a foolproof onboarding system and a guide for pretty much everything, so you don't need to do the explaining in the first place. Evidently, some smaller jobs you may not have guides for, as they are a one-off. In that case, take the time to explain as best you can what you need done and how you need it done, maybe providing an example of a comparable finished article.

However, if you find you have to correct/remind someone more than three times, it's likely to continue. In outsourcing, this is a prime example of the type of working relationship you should end sooner rather than later. Count your losses and return to the marketplace for a replacement.

Language barriers

In a global team with diversity in culture and language, people will have different ways of talking, writing and communicating. It can be hard for a non-native English speaker to comprehend everything spoken or written by a native speaker. The native speakers might use idioms, slang and colloquialisms, which can be misunderstood by the non-native speakers. Therefore, guidelines for language use is necessary in a multilingual team.

Encourage your team to use simple words and terminologies when communicating with each other. Ask your native speakers to speak slowly with your non-native speakers and avoid using any difficult words, phrases or colloquialisms. Phrases like 'Are we on the same page?', 'That looks like a dog's dinner' and 'That's a little skew-whiff' can all be easily translation in lost.

Depending on your own background, language and culture, people's mannerisms can surprise you. For example, in a chat with a freelancer from Eastern Europe or Asia, you may find as you are talking through a project or fine-tuning work the freelancer has done, that they will reply with the word 'Wait.' Now, in a face-to-face chat in the UK, that would be the equivalent of someone rudely thrusting their outstretched hand in your face. However, in the above cultures, it's simply the same as someone saying 'Hold on a minute please, while I check so I can give you a proper answer.' My point is, it's important not to take comments personally in text or voice conversations, especially when you are dealing with people from other countries. Very often, their 'Wait' is different from ours.

Low-context and high-context culture

The concept of low-context and high-context culture was first introduced by anthropologist, Edward T. Hall in his 1959 publication, *The Silent Language*. Later, these terms became more popular and widely used. In a diverse organisation, low-context and high-context cultures play an important role in communication, especially in a remote environment.

Low-context cultures are those where communication is direct and requires few non-verbal messages. The polar opposite is high-context culture, where a high amount of verbal communication is necessary and elements like facial expressions, tone of voice, hand gestures and body language are also important factors during communication.

While no country or region is specifically high context and low context, one is prominent in some parts of the world and another is popular in other parts of the world. For example, the UK, the USA, Canada, Germany, Denmark and Switzerland are some countries where low-context culture is widely observed. The countries/regions where high-context cultures are popular are Japan, Spain, France, China, Saudi Arabia, India, Pakistan, Africa, Brazil and more.

Communication in a low-context culture is mostly done in written form and it is task-oriented and guided by rules and standards. Low-context cultures are less expressive, prefer formality and rely on facts and evidence. High-context culture people are often highly expressive. They favour informal communication and sharing verbal messages. Low-context culture is straightforward and relies on working with procedures, while high-context culture prefers to work with personal trust. Someone from a high-context culture often prefers groups, while a person from low-context culture might prefer privacy and space.

Miscommunication can happen due to these cultural differences in your team. In a low-context culture, what is said is what is meant. But the same might not apply in a high-context culture. Something as simple as silence can also have different meanings in high-context culture. During meetings, your freelancer's silence might mean they didn't understand what you said or they are still processing what you said and thinking of an appropriate answer.

Let's take the example of the word 'yes'. Many times when working with a freelancer from India, Mexico or other high-context culture countries, you may ask if they can do something and they say yes. In a low-context country, the answer would mean that they can do the job. However, someone from a high-context culture country might instead mean that they understand what you are asking, rather than confirming they can do it. In this instance, you need to double-check their answer to be sure.

Understanding and addressing the cultural diversity in your team will help in the communication among your team. Low-context communication might be easier for you, as it is straightforward and saves time. But understanding both cultures will help you identify the difference among team members so that you can communicate accordingly, and encourage the same throughout your organisation.

NDAs and NCAs

Non-Disclosure Agreements (NDAs) are legally binding contracts used to prevent any disclosure of confidential information shared with the freelancers during the contract or any secrets that are too valuable to be shared outside the company. Non-Compete Agreements (NCAs) are legally binding contracts preventing your employees from starting a business or working for other businesses that are similar to your business, and can be regarded as your competition.

NDAs are common in many countries and many freelancers are used to being requested to sign such a document. If you have a strong NDA in place then, in case of breach of the agreement, it can be enforced by law. NCAs are less common and the enforcement of both agreements depends on the country's laws. To clarify, the enforcement of both of these agreements upon violation of agreed points is subjected to the law of the country/region that has been declared in the actual agreement.

These agreements are easier to enforce when you and the freelancer live in the same country or within the same jurisdiction. However, remote work is not bound to only one state or country. You are able to hire freelancers from all around the globe. The harsh reality that isn't much discussed is that the enforcement of these agreements ranges from difficult to impossible when you and your freelancer live in different countries. Indeed, even when you live in the same country, it can be time consuming and costly to follow through on legal action with no guarantee of success. When you hire a freelancer from a different country, you should clearly state in your NDA or NCA which country's law will apply for the enforcement in case of breach of agreed-upon points.

Prevention is always better than cure, so to prevent data theft, idea theft, or sharing of confidential information, it's best to only share relevant information and provide access to company tools and information only at the required level. Always have your freelancer work on your organisation's system and keep all the important information, files and documents separate. Provide only limited or required access to your freelancer. Also, remind your freelancer about the level of confidentiality of the shared information and ask them to mark and handle as such.

Before looking to enforce an NDA, you should ideally work within the marketplace conflict resolution system, as many of them include NDA-type clauses in their agreements and there may be penalties in the marketplace that ban a freelancer for not following agreed rules. This safeguard could be more powerful than your own NDA, as some freelancers get all of their business from a single marketplace and a ban there could result in their income disappearing.

Despite the above, I do still suggest you take advantage of the power of a strongly written agreement to help you in case of breach of trust. If you want to use an NDA or NCA, write a strong agreement without any jargon and misinterpretations and request a lawyer's advice while you are at it. Alternatively, use a specialist NDA-writing resource, of which there are many, including the team at EveryNDA who provide free and paid NDA documentation for you to use in your business.

Max from EveryNDA offers the following further insights:

An NDA is a contract that legally binds parties to confidentiality. It allows the parties involved to feel more comfortable sharing information that they would like to keep private. It's up to the parties to decide what would be considered confidential and what would not. An NDA is especially useful for businesses and entrepreneurs to keep trade secrets, and for start-ups with technological innovations to protect their confidential information while entering into discussions with potential licensees to discuss their inventions and technology.

Without these legal agreements, these discussions would be almost too difficult: you have to delicately balance the information that you provide so that enough is revealed and that these potential licensees can review your product or service or business but not too much that they would be able to steal your invention/technology/trade secrets.

Among the many uses of an NDA is the protection of 'Intellectual Property' when working with freelancers. For example, the NDA can include a clause that requires a freelancer to not only take all reasonable precautions to protect confidential information, but also not to copy or reverse-engineer such information for their own benefits.

Checkout a free sample NDA from EveryNDA.com here: https://www.everynda.com/blog/sample-non-disclosure-template/

Direct client interaction

Freelancers have a great deal of flexibility of time and freedom, as they work from their home. They are able to utilise this flexibility to win more projects, work additional hours and make more money. While this can only be positive, some mischievous freelancers may try to exploit their freedom and try and contact your client directly.

A typical work process might see you take your client's project and outsource it to your freelancer, taking your cut in the process. Meanwhile, the mischievous freelancer tries to make contact with your client with the intention of cutting out the middle man (you) and earning more. In so doing, they disregard the fact that, if it weren't for you, they would never have heard about the project in the first place.

These situations are rare, but they can occur. That's why I am giving you a heads-up to make sure you are prepared for this situation.

Be clear in your contract agreement document and any other legal papers that you work with that under no circumstances is the freelancer to contact your client directly. You need to specify clear rules on how your freelancers interact with your clients and what they should not do. Also mention the legal actions and penalties that will be enforced in case of the breach of those rules.

While this is something you should be aware of and guard against, even though you can't completely stop it from ever happening, I have not experienced this in the ten years I've been outsourcing to freelancers around the world.

I have, however, experienced it in one of my traditional businesses, where staff have tried to solicit jobs with clients to whom we provided maintenance services. I've had sales people leave to go to other companies and contact my clients, and I've even had a few technical people leave, start an identical business, contact all my clients and try to poach them.

With the exception of one client who was new and to be fair, wasn't a client we wanted to keep, all others remained our clients through those situations over a twenty-year period. That's not to say we never had clients leave, it's just that they didn't leave to go with old members of staff.

While you can protect yourself legally via NDAs, NCAs and so on, the best thing you can do and the best advice I can give you is to be proactive and build a great relationship with all of your clients. Ensure they know you are the reason they are receiving great service, ensure they know they are important to you, ensure they know the business doesn't rely on one specific member of the team. Tell them you have systems and processes in place so they get consistently good results. Take really good care of them by making them feel like they are your only client and the chance of them moving elsewhere will reduce enormously.

Firing a freelancer

Most of this book centres on hiring, but the final aspect to mention is the other side of the coin: firing. Firing an employee can be a difficult task even when they are having a negative impact on the business through poor time-keeping, not working well with others, resistance to change or not taking ownership of their responsibilities. As well as building resentment within the team, this type of employee can cause lower productivity and lost income. Worse still, they can cause good members of your team to leave your business and can even cost you clients.

Of course, it's not always their fault; you may also need to fire a freelancer due to a decrease in business or a cancelled project.

In a traditional environment, you have many things to consider when firing an employee, including notice periods, unfair dismissals, tribunals, etc. You may also have other linked concerns, such as their IT equipment, company car and other expenses you've committed to in order to support their role. Then, if your business model is to hire staff via recruitment companies, you'll have a further cost to hire their replacement.

In contrast, freelance relationships are very different. Even if they've been working for you long term, parting ways is considerably easier, faster and cleaner all round.

If you have an hourly contract, your obligation is to pay up to and when the hours have been logged. If you have a fixed-price contract, your obligation is to pay up to the next agreed milestone. It's important to be fair and ensure the freelancer has been compensated for the work done.

The obvious concern here is that a client can abuse the relationship between themselves and a freelancer. This does happen and is not the way you should work. To get the most out of your freelancers, first make sure you are a fair employer by ensuring the following:

- You are pleasant to work with
- You communicate promptly, providing adequate feedback and guidance, and don't expect your freelancer to be a mind reader
- You don't make them do more than was originally agreed in the job, or request more revisions than is reasonable
- You don't make the job take longer than it should, thus impacting on the freelancer's other commitments and earnings
- You don't take ages to approve milestones and release payments
- You don't threaten to leave a bad review as a means to get them to do extra unpaid work

Over and above simply being a decent person and working in an ethical manner, you should remember that freelancers will also have the opportunity to review you as a client at the end of each job. If you treat freelancers poorly, negative reviews will start to accumulate and you'll find it hard to secure the services of good and experienced freelancers in the future.

Most freelancers know when there isn't a good fit between you. And most will take the news surprisingly well if you deal with the situation in a fair and reasonable manner.

Conclusion

As we come to the end of the book, my hope is that you can see the value outsourcing will bring to you and your business, whether you're a one-person company or you have hundreds, thousands or hundreds of thousands of existing staff, like Microsoft.

The ability to use this system and grow your business faster, better and more profitably than traditional methods is yours for the taking. But understanding how outsourcing can benefit your business is only the starting point. Being open-minded and realising that there are unique risks involved is important in helping you take the first steps.

The issue of trust looms large in this book, and is probably one of the biggest reasons why people might not make the leap into the freelance marketplaces and systems described in this book. Realising that you likely already use some form of outsourcing may be the light bulb that helps you move forward. In a personal sense, you may already have your children taken care of by childminders, or you may employ a cleaner, a gardener or an ironing service. You trust these people with your family and your home, just as you trust an electrician or a plumber to fix the things that go wrong there. For more business-related tasks, you may already use an IT firm or an external bookkeeper or accountant to take care of your financial affairs. The step towards outsourcing as a core part of your business model is no less and no greater a risk than any of the above examples.

While you may ask for references for all the above listed people, on the marketplaces listed in this book, the freelancers' job histories, testimonials and review systems are fully transparent and there for all to see. Indeed, it's this transparency that in many cases guarantees the freelancers work hard to do the best job possible, as a single poor review can result in a real drop in job offers and resulting lack of income.

In my experience, the flexibility and other benefits you gain from this new model of recruiting and building your business far outweighs any downsides. Of course, you need to be careful, and you need to plan and progress appropriately, however, I trust you have found a good foundation for that in this book.

The best way to get started is to simply get started.

It's important to be realistic about your expectations of the freelancer or agency you will outsource to. For example, don't expect a $7 per hour virtual assistant to get up to speed on everything you need within a few days, and don't expect that person to become your marketer, blog creator or video editor. While most will list a multitude of skills or experience, you'll find that there are a few core skills they can help most with, and that should be your focus.

Hire appropriate people for the job. One of the great benefits of this model is that you don't need to hire people full time, which means you need fewer, if any, generalists. You can hire specialists for one or two hours per week, or whatever the requirement is for the tasks and projects within your business.

Remember to never confuse delegation with abdication. You need to give your freelancer the best chance of success if you're going to benefit from the experience. For that to happen, they first need the skills to do the job, whether these are existing skills or training you'll supply to them as a longer-term member of your team. They need clear guidance on what the end result should be, and you need to provide them with the information and tools they require to work towards a positive end result for you.

Keep your communication simple, clear, easy to reference, and ensure that you both have the same understanding of what is to be completed, by when, and for what fee, or at the very least an estimated fee if it's hourly work.

Business is tough, growing and managing a business is even tougher, and recent events have proved more than ever that absolutely anything can happen. While outsourcing as defined in this book isn't the answer for every business, it is a proven way to get tasks done, find specialists and experts from around the globe, build a flexible team, upscale and downscale as your needs dictate and build a business that is simpler to run, more profitable and provides a better service to your clients.

I hope you've found that *Outsourcing For Success* has given you an insight into the opportunity and that it helps you take your first step, or better steps, into the world of outsourcing. Feel free to reach out to me at kevashcroft.com with any questions or thoughts you have, and I promise to get back to you as soon as I can. Good luck!

Appendix I: Outsourceable job categories

Almost anything you can think of can be outsourced. I've listed all of these categories courtesy of Upwork.com. While this is a fairly comprehensive list, there are more that could be added!

Accounting & Consulting:
Accounting

Bookkeeping

Business Analysis

Financial Analysis & Modelling

Financial Management/CFO

HR Administration

Instructional Design

Management Consulting

Recruiting

Tax Preparation

Training & Development

Admin Support:
Data Entry

Online Research

Order Processing

Project Management

Transcription

Virtual Assistance

Customer Service:
Customer Service

Technical Support

Data Science & Analytics:
A/B Testing

Bandits

Data Analytics

Data Engineering

Data Extraction

Data Mining

Data Processing

Data Visualization

Deep Learning

Experimentation & Testing

Knowledge Representation

Machine Learning

Design & Creative:

2D Animation

3D Animation

Actor

Art Direction

Audio Editing/Post-Production

Audio Production

Brand Identity Design

Brand Strategy

Cartoonist

Creative Direction

Editorial Design

Exhibit Design

Fashion Design

Graphic Design

Illustration

Image Editing/Retouching

Motion Graphics Design

Musician

Music Composition

Music Production

Photography

Presentation Design

Scriptwriting

Social Media Strategy

Store Design

Videographer

Video Editing/Post-Production

Video Production

Vocalist

Voice Talent

VR & AR Design

Engineering & Architecture:
3D Modelling

3D Rendering

3D Visualization

Architecture

BIM Modelling

Biology

CAD

Chemical Engineering

Chemistry

Civil Engineering

Electrical Engineering

Electronic Engineering

- Energy Management & Modelling
- Engineering Tutoring
- Jewellery Design
- Landscape Design
- Oil & Gas Engineering
- Process Engineering
- Quantity Surveying
- Structural Engineering
- Sourcing & Procurement
- HVAC & MEP Design
- Hydraulics Engineering
- Industrial Design
- Interior Design
- Logistics & Supply Chain Management
- Mathematics
- Mechanical Engineering
- PCB Design
- Physics
- Product Design
- Science Tutoring
- Solar Energy
- Wind Energy

IT & Engineering:

Database Administration

DevOps Engineering

Information Security

Network Administration

Network Security

Solutions Architecture

System Administration

Systems Architecture

Systems Compliance

Systems Engineering

Legal:

Business & Corporate Law

General Counsel

Immigration Law

Intellectual Property Law

International Law

Labour & Employment Law

Paralegal

Regulatory Law

Securities & Finance Law

Tax Law

Sales & Marketing:

Business Development

Campaign Management

Community Management

Content Strategy

Digital Marketing

Email Marketing

Lead Generation

Marketing Automation

Marketing Strategy

Market Research

Public Relations

Search Engine Marketing

Search Engine Optimization

Social Media Marketing

Telemarketing

Translation:

Language Localization

Language Tutoring

Legal Translation

Medical Translation

Technical Translation

Translation

Web, Mobile & Software Development:
AR/VR Development

Automation QA

Back-End Development

CMS Customization

CMS Development

Database Development

Desktop Software Development

Ecommerce Development

Emerging Tech

Firmware Development

Front-End Development

Full Stack Development

Functional QA

Game Development

Mobile App Development

Mobile Design

Mobile Game Development

Product Management

Prototyping

Scripting & Automation

Scrum Master

User Research

UX/UI Design

Web Design

Writing:
Business Writing

Career Coaching

Content Writing

Copywriting

Creative Writing

Editing & Proofreading

Ghostwriting

Grant Writing

Technical Writing

Appendix II: Further freelance marketplaces

The following freelance marketplaces didn't make it into my Top Twenty list in Chapter 3, but they may be worth your investigation. As you can imagine, new marketplaces launch on a regular basis. You can find the up-to-date list on kevashcroft.com.

Aquent (staffing agency) - https://aquent.com/

Amazon Mechanical Turk (MTurk) - https://www.mturk.com/

Bark (not remote jobs, only local) -

https://www.bark.com/en/gb/

Behance (showcase of creatives around the world) -

https://www.behance.net/

Belay Solutions (similar to Zirtual) –

https://belaysolutions.com/

Boldly (Staffing business) - https://boldly.com/

Clarity.fm (consultation marketplace) - https://clarity.fm/

craigslist (job board) - https://london.craigslist.org/

CollegeRecruiter (to hire college students or freshers) -

https://www.collegerecruiter.com/

CrowdSource (job board) - https://www.crowdsource.com/

Designhill (high-quality designs from designers and artists) -

https://www.designhill.com/

Dice (job board) - https://www.dice.com/

Dribbble (discover and connect with designers worldwide) - https://dribbble.com

Freelance Writing Gigs (daily 10+ writing gigs) - https://www.freelancewritinggigs.com/

Gigster (marketplace for coders) - https://gigster.com/

Glassdoor (job board) - https://www.glassdoor.com/

Hireable (job board) - https://hireable.com/

Hiremymom (for work-from-home mums) - https://www.hiremymom.com/

Hubstaff Talent - https://talent.hubstaff.com/

Indeed (job board) - https://www.indeed.com/

Jooble (Job search engine) - https://jooble.org/

LinkedIn Profinder - https://business.linkedin.com/grow/profinder

Monster (job board) - https://www.monster.com/

Nexxt (job board) - https://www.nexxt.com/

Onlinejobs.ph (Philippines freelance market) - https://www.onlinejobs.ph/

Outsourcely (for long-term remote workers) - https://www.outsourcely.com/

PEforhire (to hire professional engineers, US based) - https://www.peforhire.com/

Penji (on-demand design service) - https://penji.co/

Pro Blogger - https://problogger.com/

Project4hire - https://project4hire.co/

Remote.com (job board + HR solution) - https://remote.com/

RemoteOK.io (job board) - https://remoteok.io/

Remotive.io (job board) - https://remotive.io/

Simply Hired (job board and HR tools) - https://www.simplyhired.com/

Sologigs (US company jobs: one individual company posts multiple jobs) – https://www.sologig.com/

Storetasker (design, development and marketing services) – https://storetasker.com/

TaskRabbit (not remote jobs - real live people helping you at your home or business) - https://www.taskrabbit.com/

Time etc (similar to Zirtual) - https://web.timeetc.com/virtualassistant/

TopCoder (design, development, data science and AI services) - https://www.topcoder.com/

The Muse (job board) - https://www.themuse.com/

Valilly (recruitment solution and automation) - https://valilly.com/

Weworkremotely - https://weworkremotely.com/

Workable (recruitment solution) - https://www.workable.com/

Working Nomads (job board) - https://www.workingnomads.co/jobs

Zeerk (similar to Fiverr) - https://zeerk.com/

ZipRecruiter (job board) - https://www.ziprecruiter.com/

Appendix III: Tools of the Trade

A single business can require a lot of software applications and tools to operate. Some tools are common and used in almost every mainstream business, while others are specific to a business. With the advances of cloud storage and sharing, project and team management is made simpler with tools that are developed to fulfil that purpose. From productivity, collaboration and communication to training and entertainment, and from time tracking and appointment scheduling tools to CRM systems, VPN and invoicing solutions, there are tools and software available for almost all of your business needs.

Before venturing into the outsourcing world, you should make a list of what you need for each of your business requirements and ensure you have either your own guides created for them that your team can follow, or use the generic guides already prepared by the developers if they cover how you will use the tools. When taking advantage of everything that outsourcing brings to you and your business, it's important to familiarise yourself with the right systems as early as possible to make your life, your freelancers' lives and your clients' results as good and as consistent as possible.

I've used a lot of these tools. Some I've started with and moved to others over time for various reasons. You need to find what suits your needs and your way of working best. The following list is not exhaustive, but it will help you get started and make progress on what's best for you.

1. **Time Tracker and Work Tracker:**
   a) Harvest - https://www.getharvest.com/
   b) TimeDoctor - https://www.timedoctor.com/
   c) Clockify - https://clockify.me/
   d) Toggl - https://toggl.com/
   e) HubStaff - https://hubstaff.com/

2. **Screenshot and Screen Recording:**
   a) Loom - https://www.loom.com/
   b) Snagit - https://www.techsmith.com/screen-capture.html
   c) Camtasia - https://www.techsmith.com/video-editor.html
   d) Windows Game Bar – Built-in Windows 10 tool
   e) Screencastify - https://www.screencastify.com/
   f) QuickTime Player for MAC - https://support.apple.com/downloads/quicktime

3. **Screen Sharing:**
   a) TeamViewer - https://www.teamviewer.com/en-us/
   b) AnyDesk - https://anydesk.com/en
   c) Zoom - https://zoom.us/

d) Skype - https://www.skype.com/en/
   e) Discord - https://discord.com/
4. **HR Management (Hiring and Recruiting):**
   a) BambooHR - https://www.bamboohr.com/
   b) Gusto - https://gusto.com/
   c) Zenefits - https://www.zenefits.com/
   d) JazzHR - https://www.jazzhr.com/
   e) Sage - https://sage.hr/
5. **Calendar and Scheduling:**
   a) Google Calendar - https://calendar.google.com
   b) Apple Calendar - https://www.icloud.com/calendar
   c) Fantastical - https://flexibits.com/fantastical
   d) Business Calendar 2 - https://www.appgenix-software.com/
   e) Calendly - https://calendly.com/
6. **Productivity and Note Keeping:**
   a) Evernote - https://evernote.com/
   b) Google Keep - https://keep.google.com
   c) Google Tasks - located at the bottom right of https://mail.google.com
   d) Google Boomerang Chrome extension -

https://chrome.google.com/webstore/detail/boomerang-for-gmail/mdanidgdpmkimeiiojknlnekblgmpdll?hl=en

e) Todoist - https://todoist.com/

f) Any.do - https://www.any.do/

g) Microsoft OneNote - https://www.microsoft.com/en-ww/microsoft-365/onenote/digital-note-taking-app

7. **Task, Project and Team Management:**

   a) Asana - https://asana.com/

   b) Trello - https://trello.com/

   c) BaseCamp - https://basecamp.com/

   d) Teamwork - https://www.teamwork.com/

   e) Monday.com - https://monday.com/

   f) Jira - https://www.atlassian.com/software/jira

8. **Password Sharing and Management:**

   a) LastPass - https://www.lastpass.com/

   b) Dashlane - https://www.dashlane.com/

   c) Bitwarden - https://bitwarden.com/

   d) Keeper - https://www.keepersecurity.com/

   e) 1Password - https://1password.com/

9. **File Storage and Sharing:**

a) Google Drive - https://drive.google.com

b) Dropbox - https://www.dropbox.com/

c) Microsoft OneDrive - https://www.microsoft.com/en/microsoft-365/onedrive/online-cloud-storage

d) iCloud Drive - https://www.icloud.com/iclouddrive

e) WeTransfer - https://wetransfer.com/

10. **File Encryption and Storage:**

a) Folder Lock - https://www.newsoftwares.net/download/

b) AxCrypt - https://axcrypt.net/

c) VeraCrypt - https://www.veracrypt.fr/en/Home.html

d) 7-Zip - https://www.7-zip.org/

11. **Communication Channel:**

a) Slack - https://slack.com/

b) Skype - https://www.skype.com/en/

c) Discord - https://discord.com/

d) WhatsApp - https://www.whatsapp.com/

e) Zoho - https://www.zoho.com/cliq/

12. **Mailing Platform:**

a) Gmail (G Suite) - https://mail.google.com/

b) Microsoft Outlook (Office 365) - https://outlook.live.com/owa/

c) Tutanota - https://tutanota.com/

d) Apple Mail - https://www.icloud.com/mail

13. **Webinar, Meeting and Conference:**
    a) Google Meet - https://meet.google.com
    b) Google Hangouts - https://hangouts.google.com/
    c) Zoom - https://zoom.us/
    d) Discord - https://discord.com/
    e) GoToWebinar - https://www.gotomeeting.com/webinar
    f) Skype - https://www.skype.com/en/

14. **Content Writing, Editing, Spelling and Grammar Check:**
    a) Google Docs - https://docs.google.com/
    b) Grammarly - https://www.grammarly.com/
    c) Scrivener - https://www.literatureandlatte.com/scrivener/overview
    d) ProWritingAid - https://prowritingaid.com/
    e) Hemingway Editor - http://www.hemingwayapp.com/

15. **Graphic Design:**
    a) Canva - https://www.canva.com/
    b) Sketch - https://www.sketch.com/
    c) Adobe Creative Cloud - https://www.adobe.com/creativecloud.html
    d) Google Charts - https://developers.google.com/chart
    e) Promo - https://promo.com/
    f) Animoto - https://animoto.com/
    g) Powtoon - https://www.powtoon.com/
    h) Affinity Designer - https://affinity.serif.com/en-us/designer/
    i) Inkscape - https://inkscape.org/

16. **Stock Images:**
    a) Unsplash - https://unsplash.com/
    b) Shutterstock - https://www.shutterstock.com/
    c) Pixabay - https://pixabay.com/
    d) Gratisography - https://gratisography.com/
    e) Pexels - https://www.pexels.com/
    f) iStockphoto - https://www.istockphoto.com/
    g) Alamy - https://www.alamy.com/

17. **Form, Survey and Questionnaire:**

a) Google Forms - https://docs.google.com/forms/

b) SurveyMonkey - https://www.surveymonkey.com/

c) Typeform - https://www.typeform.com/

d) WPForms (Plugin for WordPress) - https://wpforms.com/

e) Microsoft Forms - https://www.microsoft.com/en-us/microsoft-365/online-surveys-polls-quizzes

f) Gravity Forms (Plugin for WordPress) - https://www.gravityforms.com/

18. **Customer Relationship Management (CRM):**

    a) HubSpot - https://www.hubspot.com/

    b) Freshworks - https://www.freshworks.com/

    c) Salesforce - https://www.salesforce.com/ap/

    d) Agile - https://www.agilecrm.com/

    e) Microsoft Dynamics 365 - https://dynamics.microsoft.com/en-us/

    f) Zoho - https://www.zoho.com/crm/

19. **Customer Service and Help Desk:**

    a) Zendesk - https://www.zendesk.com/

    b) Freshdesk - https://freshdesk.com/

    c) LiveAgent - https://www.liveagent.com/

    d) HelpCrunch - https://helpcrunch.com/

e) Help Scout - https://www.helpscout.com/
   f) Zoho Desk - https://www.zoho.com/desk/
20. **Email Marketing and Automation:**
   a) Mailchimp - https://mailchimp.com/
   b) ActiveCampaign - https://www.activecampaign.com/
   c) Drip - https://www.drip.com/
   d) Constant Contact - https://www.constantcontact.com/
   e) GetResponse - https://getresponse.com/
21. **Email Management:**
   a) Google Boomerang Chrome extension - https://chrome.google.com/webstore/detail/boomerang-for-gmail/mdanidgdpmkimeiiojknlnekblgmpdll?hl=en
   b) MixMax - https://www.mixmax.com/
   c) Mailbird - https://www.getmailbird.com/
   d) Spark - https://sparkmailapp.com/
   e) Unroll.me - https://unroll.me/
22. **Bookkeeping, Accounting and Invoicing:**
   a) QuickBooks - https://quickbooks.intuit.com/global/
   b) Xero - https://www.xero.com/

- c) FreshBooks - https://www.freshbooks.com/
- d) Wave Accounting - https://www.waveapps.com/
- e) Sage - https://www.sage.com/en-us/sage-business-cloud/accounting/
- f) KashFlow - https://www.kashflow.com/

23. **Payment Processing:**
    - a) PayPal - https://www.paypal.com/
    - b) Stripe - https://stripe.com/
    - c) Square - https://squareup.com/us/en/payments
    - d) Mint - https://mint.intuit.com/
    - e) Payoneer - https://www.payoneer.com/
    - f) TransferWise - https://transferwise.com/

24. **Content Management System (CMS):**
    - a) WordPress - https://wordpress.org/
    - b) Drupal - https://www.drupal.org/
    - c) Wix - https://www.wix.com/
    - d) SquareSpace - https://www.squarespace.com/
    - e) Joomla! - https://www.joomla.org/

25. **E-commerce and Membership:**
    - a) WooCommerce - https://woocommerce.com/
    - b) Shopify - https://www.shopify.com/
    - c) Kajabi - https://kajabi.com/

d) Magento - https://magento.com/

e) BigCommerce - https://www.bigcommerce.com/

26. **Website Hosting:**

    a) WordPress Support Specialists - https://www.wpsupportspecialists.com/

    b) Bluehost - https://www.bluehost.com/

    c) Hostinger - https://www.hostinger.com/

    d) Hostgator - https://www.hostgator.com/

    e) GoDaddy - https://www.godaddy.com/

    f) DreamHost - https://www.dreamhost.com/

    g) WP Engine - https://wpengine.com/

27. **Video Hosting:**

    a) Vimeo - https://vimeo.com/

    b) Wistia - https://wistia.com/

    c) YouTube - https://www.youtube.com/

    d) Vidyard - https://www.vidyard.com/

    e) Uscreen - https://www.uscreen.tv/

28. **Search Engine Optimisation (SEO):**

    a) Semrush - https://www.semrush.com/

    b) Ahrefs - https://ahrefs.com

    c) WooRank - https://www.woorank.com/

    d) Ubersuggest - https://neilpatel.com/ubersuggest/

e) MozBar - https://moz.com/products/pro/seo-toolbar
f) Google Analytics - https://analytics.google.com/
g) Google Search Console - https://search.google.com/search-console/
h) Yoast SEO (Plugin for WordPress) - https://yoast.com/wordpress/plugins/seo/

29. Content Marketing:
   a) BuzzSumo - https://buzzsumo.com/
   b) CoSchedule - https://coschedule.com/
   c) ContentCal - https://www.contentcal.io/
   d) Uberflip - https://www.uberflip.com/
   e) Contently - https://contently.com/
   f) Skyword - https://www.skyword.com/

30. Conversion Rate Optimisation (CRO):
   a) Google Optimize - https://marketingplatform.google.com/about/optimize/
   b) Google PageSpeed Insights - https://developers.google.com/speed/pagespeed/insights/
   c) OptinMonster - https://optinmonster.com/
   d) Unbounce - https://unbounce.com/

e) Sumo/SumoMe - https://sumo.com/
   f) OptimizePress (Plugin for WordPress) - https://www.optimizepress.com/
   g) Hotjar - https://www.hotjar.com/
   h) Crazy Egg - https://www.crazyegg.com/

31. **Social Media Marketing and Management:**
    a) Hootsuite - https://www.hootsuite.com/
    b) Buffer - https://buffer.com/
    c) Sprout Social - https://sproutsocial.com/
    d) MeetEdgar - https://meetedgar.com/
    e) Later - https://later.com/
    f) Sendible - https://www.sendinblue.com/
    g) Agorapulse - https://www.agorapulse.com/

32. **Paid Advertising:**
    a) Google AdWords - https://ads.google.com/
    b) Google AdSense - https://www.google.com/adsense/start/
    c) Bing Ads - https://ads.microsoft.com/
    d) Social Media Advertising (Facebook, LinkedIn, Twitter, Instagram)
    e) Outbrain - https://www.outbrain.com/
    f) AdEspresso - https://adespresso.com/

g) WordStream Advisor - https//wordstream.com

33. **Affiliate Marketing:**
    a) ClickBank - https://www.clickbank.com/
    b) Shopify Affiliate Program - https://www.shopify.com/affiliates
    c) Amazon Associates - https://affiliate-program.amazon.com/
    d) Affiliate Window(AWIN) - https://www.awin.com/
    e) CJ Affiliate - https://www.cj.com/

34. **Market Research and Analytics:**
    a) Google Analytics - https://analytics.google.com/
    b) Google Trends - https://trends.google.com/
    c) Google Alerts - https://www.google.com/alerts
    d) Google UTM Builder - https://ga-dev-tools.appspot.com/campaign-url-builder/
    e) BuzzSumo - https://buzzsumo.com/
    f) Hotjar - https://www.hotjar.com/
    g) Crazy Egg - https://www.crazyegg.com/
    h) SiteProfiler - https://siteprofiler.com/
    i) Social Mention - http://www.socialmention.com/
    j) Statista - https://www.statista.com/
    k) Kissmetrics - https://www.kissmetrics.io/

35. **Blogs, Forums and Podcasts:**
    a) Entrepreneurs on Fire - https://www.eofire.com/
    b) Clarity.fm - https://clarity.fm/
    c) Hacker News - https://news.ycombinator.com/
    d) Quora - https://www.quora.com/
    e) Reddit - https://www.reddit.com/
    f) Stack Overflow - https://stackoverflow.com/
36. **Training and Courses:**
    a) Coursera - https://www.coursera.org/
    b) Udemy - https://www.udemy.com/
    c) edX - https://www.edx.org/
    d) Skillshare - https://www.skillshare.com/
    e) Udacity - https://www.udacity.com/
    f) LinkedIn Learning - https://www.linkedin.com/learning/
37. **VPN:**
    a) ExpressVPN - https://www.expressvpn.com/
    b) NordVPN - https://nordvpn.com/
    c) Surfshark - https://surfshark.com/
    d) IPVanish - https://www.ipvanish.com/
38. **Anti-virus:**

a) Bitdefender Plus - https://www.bitdefender.com/solutions/antivirus.html

b) Kaspersky - https://www.kaspersky.co.in/antivirus

c) Norton 360 - https://us.norton.com/360

d) Avira Prime - https://www.avira.com/en/prime

39. G-Suite and Other Google Apps:

a) Google Drive - https://drive.google.com

b) Google Docs - https://docs.google.com/

c) Google Sheets - https://docs.google.com/spreadsheets/

d) Google Slides - https://docs.google.com/presentation/

e) Google Calendar - https://calendar.google.com

f) Google Keep - https://keep.google.com

g) Google Analytics - https://analytics.google.com/

h) Google Search Console - https://search.google.com/search-console/

i) Google AdWords - https://ads.google.com/

j) Google PageSpeed Insights - https://developers.google.com/speed/pagespeed/insights/

k) Google Keyword Planner - me/tools/keyword-planner/

h) Google AdSense - https://www.google.com/adsense/start/

l) Google Forms - https://docs.google.com/forms/

m) Google Charts - https://developers.google.com/chart

n) Google Meet - https://meet.google.com

40. Microsoft Office 365:

a) Microsoft Word - https://www.microsoft.com/en-us/microsoft-365/word

b) Microsoft Excel - https://www.microsoft.com/en-us/microsoft-365/excel

c) Microsoft PowerPoint - https://www.microsoft.com/en/microsoft-365/powerpoint

d) Microsoft Outlook - https://www.microsoft.com/en-us/microsoft-365/outlook/email-and-calendar-software-microsoft-outlook

e) Microsoft OneDrive - https://www.microsoft.com/en/microsoft-365/onedrive/online-cloud-storage
f) Microsoft OneNote - https://www.microsoft.com/en-ww/microsoft-365/onenote/digital-note-taking-app?ms.url=onenotecom&rtc=1
g) Microsoft Teams - https://www.microsoft.com/en/microsoft-teams/group-chat-software
h) Microsoft To Do - https://todo.microsoft.com/

41. All-in-one Solutions:

a) Zoho - https://www.zoho.com/
b) Zapier - https://zapier.com/
c) IFTTT - https://ifttt.com/
d) Automate.io - https://automate.io/

Acknowledgements

I couldn't have completed this book without the help of some people I'd like to give a shout-out to.

A.J. Lawrence of The JAR Group has been doubly generous with both his case study and example job description, and I'd also like to thank Matt Harrison, VP of Strategy at FreeUp, and George Papadeas, COO of The HOTH, for their assistance with the FreeUp case study.

Thanks to Max from EveryNDA for providing extra information on NDAs and a link to a free downloadable agreement.

My virtual assistant, Pratik Khanal, for various bits of research: you've been a great help all the way through this process.

My BETA readers who all provided their time and some valuable feedback: Brian Williamson, David Frame and Sean Connaughton – thank you so much.

To my wonderful editor, Bryony Sutherland: who would have thought that a chance meeting twenty years ago in St Lucia would have resulted in you editing my first book!

To my beautiful wife, Joan, and crazy kids, Robbie and April: thank you for all your love each and every day.

About the Author

Kev Ashcroft started his first business at nineteen years of age, back when it wasn't fashionable to be an entrepreneur, especially at that age. He's been involved in every area of starting and growing businesses from planning, admin, technical, sales, marketing, HR, funding and equity pitches, to preparing for and completing a business sale.

Over the years he has mentored at Project Scotland, Strathclyde University, Entrepreneurial Spark and with private clients. Kev exited his long-term IT business in 2011 after selling to a UK telecoms PLC. In 2017 he relocated from Scotland to Spain to start a new chapter with his wife and kids. He continues to start new businesses and grow existing companies using outsourced teams, while advising others on the benefits of the freelance world.

He's made a lot of great decisions and a few bad ones that you often learn more from. These have led to a wealth of experience and understanding of the journey we entrepreneurs are on and how to make it easier than it often appears. He now provides the benefit of his battle scars so that you can enjoy your journey as an entrepreneur or business owner, avoiding many common pitfalls along the way.

If you'd like to find out more about how Kev can help you make your business a success through outsourcing, mentoring or coaching, please contact him using the details below. He'd love to hear from you, halve your problems, and get you moving faster than you ever thought possible.

The simplest way to get in touch is to visit kevashcroft.com, where you'll find further information on outsourcing, comprehensive guides, options to book a call or consultation should you wish to fast-track your outsourcing journey, or to completely outsource your outsourcing!

You'll find regular blogs and articles on outsourcing and the option to add your details to get regular updates and advice/tips sent direct to your inbox.

One final little ask: if you've found this book useful, please head to the link below to leave a review and rating. Every little helps and hopefully, by spreading the word, more people can benefit from outsourcing as a way to spread the load, reduce stress, find great people, build awesome relationships, grow your business, and service your clients in the best way possible.

Printed in Great Britain
by Amazon